HALDANE'S BEST ANSWERS TO TOUGH INTERVIEW QUESTIONS

Books in the Haldane's Best Series...

HALDANE'S BEST ANSWERS TO TOUGH INTERVIEW QUESTIONS

Bernard Haldane Associates

IMPACT PUBLICATIONS
Manassas Park, Virginia

Liability/Warranty: The author and publisher have made every attempt to provide the reader with accurate information. However, given constant changes in the employment field, they make no claims that this information will remain accurate at the time of reading. Furthermore, this information is presented for information purposes only. The author and publisher make no claims that using this information will guarantee the reader a job. The author and publisher shall not be liable for any loss or damages incurred in the process of following the advice presented in this book.

Library of Congress Cataloging-in-Publication Data

Haldane's best answers to tough interview questions / Bernard Haldane Associates.
  p. cm.
Includes index.
ISBN 1-57023-111-7 (alk. paper)
  1. Employment interviewing. I. Bernard Haldane Associates.

HF5549.5.I6 H33 1999
650.14—dc21   99-049229
                                          CIP

All names contained herein are fictitious and are not intended to represent any real people or organizations. Any resemblance to real persons or organizations is purely coincidental.

Publisher: For information on Impact Publications, including current and forthcoming publications, authors, press kits, bookstore, and submission requirements, visit Impact's Web site: *www.impactpublications.com*

Publicity/Rights: For information on publicity, author interviews, and subsidiary rights, contact the Public Relations and Marketing Department: Tel. 703/361-7300 or Fax 703/335-9486.

Sales/Distribution: Bookstore sales are handled through Impact's trade distributor: National Book Network, 15200 NBN Way, Blue Ridge Summit, PA 17214, Tel. 1-800-462-6420. All other sales and distribution inquiries should be directed to the publisher: Sales Department, IMPACT PUBLICATIONS, 9104 Manassas Dr., Suite N, Manassas Park, VA 20111-5211, Tel. 703/361-7300, Fax 703/335-9486, or *haldane@impactpublications.com*

Book design by Kristina Ackley
Layout by Stacy Noyes

Contents

DON'T JUST CHANGE YOUR JOB; CHANGE YOUR LIFE™

I am pleased you are joining us on what may well become an exciting journey, and a defining moment in your career and your life—finding a new job or career based upon your interview skills.

Like other books in the "Haldane's Best" series, this is not your typical job search book. It represents the collective efforts of hundreds of career professionals who have worked with over 600,000 clients during the past 50+ years in preparing them for the critical referral and job interviews. Experienced in the day-to-day realities of finding jobs and changing careers, our work continues to represent the cutting edge of career management. Indeed, we have pioneered the referral interview and developed many innovative interview techniques that are now standard practices among career advisors. If you follow the advice outlined in this book, you should be able to land the right job for you.

I also invite you to contact our offices in the United States, Canada, and the United Kingdom. Consisting of a network of more than 80 career management offices, Bernard Haldane Associates works with thousands of clients each day in conducting effective job searches based upon the many principles outlined in the "Haldane's Best" series. We include contact information on the offices nearest you in the Appendix (pages 189–197) as well as on our Web site: *www.jobhunting.com.*

Please join us as we celebrate more than 50 years of helping hundreds of thousands of professionals realize their career dreams. May your next interview result in an exciting change in your career and your life!

Jerold Weinger
Chairman of the Board and CEO
Bernard Haldane Associates

HALDANE'S BEST ANSWERS TO TOUGH INTERVIEW QUESTIONS

JOB INTERVIEWS GET JOBS

If you think resumes, letters, and Internet job searching get jobs, think again. These job search activities are prerequisites to getting a job interview. Indeed, the job interview is the single most important step in the job search process. No interview, no job offer. Do well during the job interview, and you may be offered the job. Do poorly during the job interview, and the door may permanently close behind you.

So how can you best prepare for interviews that lead to job offers? What types of interviews will you encounter? What questions are you most likely to be asked? Do you know how to best respond to different types of questions? What questions are you prepared to ask? How well do you communicate nonverbally? How can you best influence the hiring decision after the job interview? Can you negotiate a higher salary?

LESSONS FROM EXPERIENCE

Since a job interview is the single most important prerequisite to a job offer, you simply must do well in the interview. Fortunately, a great deal has been written about the "do's" and "don'ts" of job interviews. Not surprisingly, most books focus on sample questions and answers to the most frequently asked interview questions. Others include examples of questions the interviewee also should ask. Overall, few books include interview strategies that relate to other stages in the job search, especially self-assessment, research, networking, and resume and letter writing.

This is a very different interview book. It combines interview strategies with examples of interview questions that should be both answered and asked during two different types of job search interviews—referral interviews and job interviews. Based on more than 50 years of experience in working with more than 600,000 clients, we at Bernard Haldane Associates have learned a great deal about what works and doesn't work for job seekers. In the following pages we share with you the many lessons and secrets of conducting interviews that result in job offers and renewed career success for hundreds of our clients each day. We present interview strategies, as well as examples of interview questions and answers, that truly reflect the job search experiences of our clients. While our clients disproportionately represent professionals earning in excess of $50,000 a year, with many being executives earning well into six figures, the interview strategies and examples we present here are applicable to most job search situations. Indeed, individuals first entering the job market should find valuable advice to assist them in preparing for both referral and job interviews.

INTERVIEWS IN YOUR JOB SEARCH

Interviews play a critical role at various stages of your job search. They help determine whether or not you are "qualified" for the position in question. But being "qualified" means different things to different people, including interviewees and interviewers.

At Bernard Haldane Associates, our clients always do first things first by following a well-developed sequential set of job search activities that function as prerequisites for landing job interviews:

- Conduct a thorough self-assessment using the Myers-Briggs Type Indicator and Success Factor Analysis
- Formulate a targeted objective
- Conduct research
- Write resumes and letters
- Network

These job search steps are outlined in our companion volume, *Haldane's Best Resumes For Professionals.* While many of these steps are relatively passive activities—conducted alone or with the assistance of a career professional—networking and interviewing are the critical **interpersonal** dimensions of the job search. Going beyond writing and telephone skills, networking and interviewing ultimately involve interaction and face-to-face communication with potential employers. Encompassing both verbal and nonverbal communication, with the nonverbal predominating, job interviews involve a two-way flow of communication in which the participants exchange information and identify clues in order to determine whether or not they want to work together, or if they are "fit" for each other.

One of the great job search myths is that the purpose of the job interview is to determine your **qualifications** through a process of asking and answering questions. If this were true, employers would dispense with costly job interviews and rely on more valid screening activities, such as tests, demonstrations, and questionnaires. The truth is that job interviews have little to do with determining qualifications, experience, or talent. These qualifiers have already been determined, through pre-screening activities, prior to receiving an invitation to a job interview. Since you already pre-qualify for a job interview— you have the requisite experience and talent to do the job based on your resume and other credentials—the job interview is more about *chemistry*, *likability*, or that *gut feeling* that the candidate is right for the job and organization. In other words, do both you and the interviewer like each other enough to want

> *Job interviews have little to do with determining qualifications, experience, or talent. They're more about chemistry, likability, or that gut feeling that the candidate is right for the job and organization.*

to work together in the long term? Are you likely to fit into the organizational culture given your personality and style? Such nonverbal elements as how you dress, speak, smile, sit, maintain eye contact, use vocal inflections, and even eat are usually more important in determining job interview outcomes than the actual content of your answers and the quality of your questions. Ultimately you'll be offered the job because the employer *likes* you more than other candidates.

Therefore, how you communicate your likability, as well as your qualifications, during the job interview will largely determine whether or not you will be offered the job. Knowing this, you should pay particular attention to the nonverbal messages you are likely to send during the job interview. The very first messages occur during the first five seconds when an interviewer sees how you dress and groom for the interview and how you greet the interviewer. Do you look, feel, and sound great for both the position and the organization?

While the job interview is the ultimate goal of such job search activities, it is not the only interview that should take place during the job search. As part of the networking process, our clients also develop powerful **referral interviewing skills** which aim at eliciting important job information, advice, and referrals that ultimately lead to job interviews and offers. Referral interviews play a central role in determining whether or not an individual is the perfect "fit" for a job. In many respects, referral interviews may be more important to landing a job than actual job interviews! As you will see in the remainder of this book, both referral and job interviews go hand in hand. You must be skilled in handling both types of interviews.

PREPARE FOR THE PERFECT INTERVIEW

You've probably heard the maxim oft repeated by realtors that the three things that count the most when selling a house are location, location, and location. Haldane Advisors share a similar maxim with their clients. Indeed, the three things that count the most when selling yourself in a job interview is preparation, preparation, and more preparation. The homeowner can't change the location of his or her house to make it more marketable, but you can do everything to make yourself more marketable in a job interview.

Preparing for job interviews is some of the hardest work you will ever do. But the payoff—not just a job offer—but the right job for you, is your reward. And what happens if you don't prepare adequately for your job interviews? You don't get the job offer? Probably not getting the job offer is one result, but that's just for starters. The negative ramifications are far more numerous and pervasive than just not being offered the job. In addition:

- You waste your time going to the interview.
- You waste the interviewer's time.

■ You nullify any likelihood of being considered for any other position at a later time by this interviewer or this company.

■ You create a situation in which negative comments about your interview (translate: negative comments about your skills, knowledge and abilities) are networked to other employers who may be of interest to you in the future.

So the truth is that you cannot afford to take shortcuts on any of the steps necessary to prepare for each and every job interview. If the interview is not worth enough to you to put in the necessary time to prepare adequately, then the job is not worth getting. If the job is not worth getting, why waste your time and the interviewer's?

Preparation will be a frequent theme running through this entire book. For if you are well prepared in every aspect of "interview readiness" you are at least 90 percent of the way to getting a job offer before you even leave home! Even though it is the actual interview that most people are apprehensive about, your hardest work is done prior to the interview. From preparing examples of effectiveness, anticipating questions the interviewer is likely to ask you, preparing questions you want to ask the interviewer, to preparing your interview image—these are just a few of the areas in which you need to be well prepared. If you have prepared thoroughly, you can walk into your interview relatively calm and completely confident. Just as the most important work a basketball player does is before he runs onto the court or a concert violinist's hardest work is prior to walking onto the stage, the most important part of your winning the job offer is done **before** you walk into the interview!

Do You Work to Live or Live to Work?

T.G.I.F.—"Thank goodness it's Friday!" How many times have you heard it? How many times have you said it? How often do you hear T.G.I.M.—"Thank goodness it's Monday?" For most people, going to work is a chore, but we look forward to the weekend when we can do what we want. What does this say about our attitudes toward our jobs? What if you could look forward to going to work each day with the same zest and anticipation you feel for the weekend? Yes, we know some people do. But we think they are the exception. Steven Spielberg is excited about his work, but he is a famous movie producer. How can someone feel passionate about managing a cellular phone company, doing corporate training, or consulting with major manufacturing firms?

Take almost any job, and if you look far enough, you will find someone who really likes and feels fulfilled doing that job. The problem isn't in the work, it lies in the **fit**—either good or bad—between the job and the person doing it. Talk to people about how they chose their careers and the most common answers are likely to be:

> *Your hardest work is done prior to the interview. If you have prepared thoroughly, you can walk into your interview relatively calm and completely confident.*

- I knew my dad wanted me to follow in his footsteps and take over the family business someday.

- I knew my mother always wanted me to be a doctor.

- I always heard that teaching was a good field for women.

- I knew there were lots of jobs in computers.

- I knew I could always get a job if I went into nursing.

These individuals tried to fit into jobs that met other people's expectations or where they thought employment opportunities were good. They tried to fit into jobs rather than find a job that was fit for them!

Bernard Haldane Associates stresses the importance of job fit. Trying to fit into jobs with numerous perceived opportunities or ones recommended by well-meaning friends or family is a sure path to job dissatisfaction and frustration. You need to enjoy your work. Most people spend the major part of their waking hours at work. If you don't enjoy your work, eventually you'll just put in time and go through the motions. Eventually you'll put the blame for your job dissatisfaction on the particular job—rather than the type of work you are doing—or blame the people you work with for your discontent. So you find another job and assume that your problems are solved, only to find that with time the new job provides no greater fulfillment than the previous one. Many people never break out of the circle of misemployment.

This cycle of misemployment should not and need not happen to you. The Haldane approach to career building is to coach each individual to identify his or her strengths and then help those individuals to identify and find jobs that are fulfilling to them. Genuine motivation comes from within you—not from your mother's aspirations for you or your employer's admonitions to do better work. If you have work that is fulfilling, work that you enjoy, work that allows you to use your strengths, you will be motivated. You can wake up on Monday morning looking forward to the weekdays ahead.

Benefit From the Haldane Approach and Network

While the information in this book will help you conduct referral and job interviews on your own, at the same time, you may want to take advantage of the Bernard Haldane Associates network of support services which consists of hundreds of career professionals, called Career Advisors, in more than 80 offices in the United States, Canada, and the United Kingdom (see the Appendix for a complete listing of this network of offices). Anyone can conduct a job search on his or her own and find a job. But we assume you don't want to find just any job. You want a high quality job that is the right "fit" for both you and the employer—one you really enjoy doing and one that benefits both you and the employer. Unfortunately, the novice do-it-yourself approach often results in taking shortcuts rather than doing first things first. For example, most job seekers begin their job search by first writing their resume rather than doing the necessary foundation work that should be the basis for their resume and other key job search activities, such as networking, interviewing, and negotiating. After all, they say, isn't that what you're supposed to do first, because that's what others always do? Some, as indicated by the popularity of resume example books, even go so far as to creatively plagiarize others' resumes. By following the crowd, they literally put the horse before the cart and thereby immediately handicap their job search with an ill-fitting resume that may communicate all the wrong messages!

You owe it to yourself to present your very best self to employers. That means taking the time and spending some money to do first things first when conducting a job search. The prerequisite foundation work involves self-assessment and goal setting—two activities that may be best done with the assistance of a professional career advisor or career coach. If you fail to do this foundation work and go directly to writing your resume and interviewing for jobs, you will most likely join thousands of other do-it-yourself job seekers who meander through the job market trying to find a job they can fit into. You will find a job but chances are it will not be a good fit. You may be well advised to work with a professional career advisor or career coach to identify what it is you do well and enjoy doing.

The Haldane approach, which also is known as Success Factor Analysis, has helped thousands of clients who use Haldane's career management services for coaching them through the job search process. With the assistance of a professional career coach who helps them with assessment, goal setting, resume writing, referral interviews, and job interviews, these individuals go on to find jobs that are excellent fits. While these same individuals could conduct a job search on their own, they choose to work with a professional who can assist them every step of the way. The professional does not find them a job. Instead, their career coach provides important career services, advice, and structure that enables the individual to become successful on his or her own terms. In the process, individuals acquire important long-term career development skills that will serve them well throughout their worklife.

Let's talk truth about what we're dealing with in the world of self-help and enlightenment. It can be very lonely and depressing out there in the job market. Our experience, as well as that of most career advisors, is that very few job seekers conduct this process well on their own. Not that they can't; it's just that they won't and thus they don't. Understanding, yes; action, some, but not enough sustained, purposeful action to make things happen the way they should. Most job seekers can cognitively understand what's involved in conducting a successful job search, but the actual process of putting it all together, finding time, implementing each step properly, remaining focused, and maintaining a high level of motivation and energy in the face of no responses or ego-wrenching rejections is something that is very difficult to do on their own. It's not surprising that people normally used to being effective all of a sudden feel ineffective when conducting their own job search. Nothing seems to work according to expectation, or perhaps expectations are either too high or are misplaced. They procrastinate, find excuses, get depressed, and give up in what is often a cycle of good intentions and dashed expectations with sustained action conspicuously absent. Indeed, very few people ever do it right on their own. Accordingly, most people can benefit tremendously by using the services of professional career advisors. A career management professional can save you a great deal of time, money, and headaches because he/she combines expertise with a structure for implementing a job search campaign. This expertise comes in many forms:

> ## Client Feedback
>
> *"Right from the beginning, Haldane's techniques helped build my self esteem, gave me direction and helped me increase my salary 100% more than my previous position with less frustration and stress than before."*
>
> **—M.H.**

- testing and assessing
- developing and targeting a job search plan
- assisting with writing resumes and letters
- honing networking skills
- implementing an action plan
- coaching for job interviews and negotiations

Most important of all, a professional can serve as a mentor who helps you maintain your focus and motivation as well as provides a critical structure for routinely implementing each phase of your job search.

At the same time, you need to be cautious in using so-called professional career services. This is a big business fraught with snake-oil salesmen and varying levels of competence. Professional career services come in many different forms, from testing and assessment centers to full-blown career marketing operations. Some individuals and companies offer career services at an hourly rate while others charge a flat contract price. If you work with someone who charges by the hour, be sure to know exactly what you need. Otherwise, you may be putting together a piece-meal job search that will most likely produce less than desirable outcomes. We prefer a contract arrangement that covers the complete job finding process, from start to finish. This type of arrangement avoids the chaos and excuses attendant with piece-meal activities; it focuses on every element in a successful job search. Above all, it commits the individual to seeing the process through at each step and doing everything possible to ensure success. Individuals use their time efficiently, remain focused, and handle well the psychological ups and downs of finding a job. Without such a long-term commitment and structure to move through the process expeditiously, individuals tend to conduct a haphazard job search, experience lots of psychological downs, and short-change their future by conducting a relatively ineffective job search.

Unfortunately, some career operations also are fraudulent. They take your money in exchange for broken promises. The promises usually come in the form of finding you a job. Many of these firms promise to do all the work for you—write your resume, broadcast it to hundreds of employers, and schedule interviews. All you have to do is write a check for this service and then sit back for the phone to ring. While this may sound good, because it appears to be a quick and easy way to find a job, such an approach is antithetical to the more than 50 years of Haldane experience.

At Bernard Haldane Associates we believe in doing first things first and coaching job seekers to do their very best. You team up with an experienced Career Advisor who literally takes you step-by-step through the complete career planning and job search process, from assessment, goal setting, researching, and resume and letter writing to networking, interviewing, and negotiating salary. Our clients also have access to Haldane's new Career Strategy 2000 electronic program. Designed specifically for Haldane's clients, this rich and powerful electronic program uses the Internet for conducting research, networking, distributing resumes, and targeting employers. We do not find you a job. That's not what we do nor should be doing for you. Instead, we help you find your own job through a well-structured process. This is an important distinction often lost in the job search business. It's a distinction that is central to writing a Haldane resume and conducting Haldane referral and job interviews that should ultimately represent the "unique you" to employers.

COMMUNICATE YOUR LIKABILITY

As you prepare for interviews, keep in mind what employers are looking for in today's job market. They first and foremost want to hire competent individuals who are qualified to take charge and produce results. Hopefully, you know what you do well and enjoy doing, you have specific goals, and you have produced Haldane-principled resumes and letters that clearly communicate your qualifications to employers as outlined in our two companion volumes: ***Haldane's Best Resumes For Professionals*** and ***Haldane's Best Cover Letters For Professionals***. Such documents should screen you in for job interviews because they tell employers that you have the requisite skills and accomplishments to do the job better than others.

In addition to knowing if you have the requisite qualifications to do the job, employers also want to hire people they like. And that's where both the referral and job interview play critical roles in getting a job. Only a foolish employer would hire someone who only demonstrates the best technical qualifications for a job. Most employers don't want high performers who are obnoxious, self-centered, and disruptive to the organization. All things being equal or near equal, the person who communicates his likability the best during the job interview will get the job. Whatever you do, don't assume your technical qualifications and experience are the key to landing a job. Your personality may be just as important, especially if you are the type of person who has excellent communication and people skills. Employers look for "chemistry" that is the key to determining how good a "fit" you are for the job and the organization.

DETERMINE YOUR
INTERVIEW READINESS

P reparation is the key to interview effectiveness. If you go to an interview without thorough preparation, don't expect to do well. You will literally cheat yourself and those involved in the interview by selling yourself short. To market yourself effectively, you simply must prepare well for the interview. To make a decision that is right for you as to whether you want to invest part of your life working for this organization depends in large measure on how well you have prepared before you go to the interview. How well you market yourself for the position—and sell yourself—depends on your advance preparation.

BEING PREPARED

Most people head off for their job interviews ill-prepared. In some cases, it is because they did not know how to prepare; in other instances, they thought they could shortcut the process. Relying on their perceived people skills and cleverness—"I have always been good at talking with people; I can bluff my way through this too"—is a mistake some make. As a result, they present themselves poorly. After a frustrating period of going for interviews and not getting job offers, they may accept the first job they are offered—even though they have a nagging feeling that this isn't a job where they want to spend their time or one that will advance their long-term career goals.

Throughout this book we will examine many areas requiring thorough preparation. Before we begin, it should be useful for you to take stock of how far along you are toward being ready for an interview. The list of statements that follows comprises what we call your "Job Interview Readiness I.Q." You should review these statements prior to each interview you have scheduled, since preparation for one interview does not guarantee readiness for another interview. The work you did to fully prepare you for one interview may only partially prepare you for the next one. After all, both the participants and the situation will change. As these elements change, additional preparation will be necessary to meet the new situation.

CHECK YOUR INTERVIEW READINESS I.Q.

If you can respond in the affirmative to each of the following statements, you should be well prepared to face the job interview. A solid, unequivocal "yes" to each statement should give you confidence that you will interview well.

1. I know what I do well and enjoy doing   Yes   No

2. I can describe to another person in a concise statement what work I want to do   Yes   No

3. I have prepared a minimum of 50 examples of my effectiveness (past accomplishments.)   Yes   No

4. I can talk specifically about what I can do for this employer by selecting the appropriate example(s) of my past accomplishments (Taken from my examples of effectiveness.)   Yes   No

5. I have kept abreast of developments in the industry in which the job I want exists by reading:

   - general news magazines (Time, U.S. News & World Report, Newsweek)   Yes   No

   - business publications (Fortune, Forbes)   Yes   No

   - industry publications specific to my targeted job   Yes   No

6. I have gathered information about the company/government agency where I will be interviewing by:

   - investigating the company/agency Website   Yes   No

   - talking with people who work there   Yes   No

■ talking with people who used to work there   Yes   No

■ keeping abreast of actions impacting the organization
(merger, downsizing, expansion, competition)   Yes   No

■ reading the community newspaper(s)   Yes   No

7. I have gathered information about the person(s) (likely to be) conducting the interview by:

■ investigating the company/agency Website   Yes   No

■ talking with people who work there   Yes   No

■ talking with people who used to work there   Yes   No

■ reading the community newspaper(s)   Yes   No

8. I have gathered information about the salary range for the position I want by:

■ conducting referral interviews with people in this
industry/region   Yes   No

■ checking salary surveys available through:

   ■ my professional association   Yes   No
   ■ the state employment commission   Yes   No
   ■ salary surveys in business publications   Yes   No
   ■ salary surveys posted on the Internet   Yes   No

9. I have anticipated questions I will most likely be asked during this job interview related to my:

■ education   Yes   No
■ skills   Yes   No
■ accomplishments   Yes   No
■ work style   Yes   No
■ supervisory style   Yes   No
■ work history/promotions   Yes   No
■ motivation   Yes   No
■ personality   Yes   No

- interaction with others   Yes   No
- strengths   Yes   No
- weaknesses   Yes   No
- unusual items on my resume/cover letter   Yes   No

10. I have strategized the jist of the responses I would make to questions I have anticipated, but I have not tried to memorize answers   Yes   No

11. I have supports for my responses to questions (examples, statistics, employer evaluations)   Yes   No

12. I have practiced talking through responses to questions, but have not memorized exact responses   Yes   No

13. I have prepared a list of questions I need to have answered by the interviewer   Yes   No

14. I have practiced talking through the questions I plan to ask the interviewer, but have not tried to memorize them   Yes   No

15. I have selected the items I will wear and carry to the interview   Yes   No

16. I know exactly how to get to the interview site   Yes   No

17. I know how long it will take to get to the interview site—on the day of the week, and at the time of day I will be making the trip   Yes   No

18. I have allowed extra time for unexpected traffic tie-ups, have checked into the parking situation, and know whether there are any security procedures that will take time as I enter the building   Yes   No

19. I know the name of the person to ask for when I arrive at the interview site, the department where the person works, and the correct extension   Yes   No

20. I have asked myself whether there is anything else
I might anticipate special to my specific situation
and if there is, I have prepared for it   Yes   No

If you were able to honestly respond with a definite "yes" to each of these statements, you have a very high readiness for your next interview. Remember to prepare just as fully and carefully for any future interviews. Your preparation for one interview only partially prepares you for your next one.

If you had a problem with either of the first two statements, you may wish to consult one of our other books—***Haldane's Best Resumes For Professionals***. The resume book provides details on how to conduct Success Factor Analysis, which addresses skills assessment, as well as how to concisely state a job objective. The remaining 18 statements are addressed in this book.

INTERVIEW MYTHS

Over our lifetimes most of us have heard a lot about the job search in general and the job interview in particular. Some of the advice is useful. However, much of it is now outdated and some may never have been productive for the job seeker. For example, many questions that might commonly have been asked in a job interview 25 years ago may be considered illegal, discriminatory, or inappropriate today. Limiting one's search to the reactive mode of responding to help wanted ads and sitting back hoping to be called for an interview was never a good job search strategy!

Let's look at several commonly held job interview myths and realities to get a better understanding of what works best. We will look in greater depth at the realities in later chapters.

MYTH #1: **Every interview in my job search will be a job interview.**

REALITY: Some of the most fruitful interviews you can engage in are referral interviews. These are interviews which you set up and conduct to gain information, advice, referrals and to be favorably remembered. Referral interviews often lead to job interviews and provide invaluable information for your later job interviews—including the process of negotiating your salary.

MYTH #2: **My resume will get me the job. If I write an excellent resume, I don't have to worry about anything else.**

REALITY: The purpose of your resume and cover letter are to get the attention of the employer and to motivate that person to want to find out more about you—invite you to an interview. You still must sell yourself in the interview which includes establishing rapport with the interviewer(s) as well as giving evidence of your accomplishments.

MYTH #3: **Once I send off my resume for a job, the only thing I can do is wait to hear from the employer.**

REALITY: Waiting is not a good job search strategy. You should attempt a proactive approach to complement your reactive application. If you have responded to an ad and mailed your resume to the personnel department, do a little sleuthing on the Internet or amongst acquaintances familiar with the company. You may be able to determine the operating department where the opening exists. If you target the head of the operating unit that has a need to fill a position, you may find yourself interviewing with that person only to go home to find a rejection letter from the human resources department! This actually happened to one of our clients!

MYTH #4: **If I get a phone call from an employer, it must mean they aren't very interested in my candidacy because they didn't take the time to reply by letter.**

REALITY: If you get a phone call from an employer after submitting your resume, you should assume it is a screening interview. Your resume piqued the employer's interest enough that he or she wants to know about you, but not enough that he or she wants to commit to a face-to-face interview yet. Always be prepared for an unexpected call that is a screening interview. You must listen carefully, keep your responses and questions focused and remember your goal is to be invited for a face-to-face interview.

MYTH #5: For the employer, the purpose of the interview is to determine if you are qualified for the job.

REALITY: The employer already has determined that you are qualified for the job before he or she invites you to the interview. The primary purpose of the interview is to determine whether or not you will fit into the organization— your personality and likability. The employer will be looking for "chemistry." In the end, the employer wants to hire someone who is both qualified and likable.

> *In the end, the employer wants to hire someone who is both qualified and likable.*

MYTH #6: My goal in a job interview is to get the job.

REALITY: Your goal is to both give and elicit information—especially if this is your first interview with this employer—and get a second interview! You want to impress the interviewer favorably so that you will remain a candidate and be called back for another of what will probably be a series of interviews, and you also want to get information as to what the employer needs. That will both help you present your accomplishments so that they demonstrate your "fit" for the particular position and help you determine if this is a job you likely will accept if it is offered.

MYTH #7: I have all the right skills and lots of experience related to this position. It's a cinch the job is as good as mine if I can just get the interview.

REALITY: Everyone invited to interview for a position is thought to have the requisite skills to do the job. What will set you apart from the others is how well you convince the interviewer(s) that you are the perfect "fit" for the job. You must communicate many qualities other than your skills and experience.

MYTH #8: I can't really do much to prepare for the interview since I don't know what questions I will be asked.

REALITY: Although you cannot know exactly what questions you will be asked, you can anticipate most of the areas they will cover. You will no doubt be asked about your accomplishments, your job progression, your personality, and if you are a recent graduate—your education. Expect to be asked questions about your strengths and weaknesses, your goals, and how you might behave in certain situations. You not only can prepare, you absolutely must prepare!

> *Expect to be asked questions about your strengths and weaknesses, your goals, and how you might behave in certain situations.*

MYTH #9: I have always been able to talk my way through anything. I'll just go into the interview and dazzle the interviewer with my verbosity.

REALITY: You may fill silence, but the verbosity will most likely come out as a "stream of consciousness" without focus. You need to be highly focused in the interview—both with your responses to questions and the targeted questions you ask. Preparation is a necessity even for those comfortable with their conversational abilities.

MYTH #10: I'll wear something to the interview that will really get their attention and make them remember me.

REALITY: If they remember you because of what you wore to the interview, it is because you stood out. If you stood out, you did not fit in as one of them. Your attire should look professional and like the people who are interviewing you. You do not want your appearance to detract from the focus of the interview which should be on your accomplishments and "fit."

MYTH #11:   **I should do most of the talking in the interview because they want to know more about me.**

REALITY: You need to talk, but you also need to ask questions of the interviewer(s) and listen to the answers. The questions you ask will provide you with information you need to determine whether this job is right for you. Your questions will also impress the interviewer if they are questions geared to determining more depth about the position and the qualities needed to excel on the job. Your talk should be focused. Avoid long rambling responses.

MYTH #12:   **Once I get into the job interview, I should take charge so the interviewer will recognize my leadership abilities.**

REALITY: In most situations this is a good way to kill your chances of being further considered for the job. In a job interview, the employer should be responsible for the structure and progression of the interview. Certainly you want to ask questions at appropriate junctures, and you may provide information that you believe will further your candidacy if it appears the interviewer is not going to ask about it. If the interviewer is particularly inept, you may subtly try to direct the line of questioning toward areas that allow you to demonstrate your strengths relative to the employer's needs. But this must be so subtle that it never appears that you have really taken control of the interview.

MYTH #13:   **It is impossible to be too confident in a job interview.**

REALITY: It is called being cocky, and unless one of the job qualifications is being obnoxious, it will not advance your candidacy. You want to appear self-assured and confident of your ability to do the job. You do not want to appear cocky.

MYTH #14:	**If I arrive late for the interview, I'll find a good excuse—I got lost or couldn't find a parking space.**
REALITY:	It is nearly impossible to recover from the negative impression made when one is late for a job interview. Employers expect you are on your best behavior for the interview. If you cannot get to the interview on time, it raises serious questions about your likelihood of getting to work on time. We know that the first five minutes of the interview are the most important; you will fail to make a good impression in the first five minutes if you are not there.

> *The first five minutes of the interview are the most important.*

MYTH #15:	**I should avoid bringing up anything in the interview that would raise questions about my qualifications or ability to do the job.**
REALITY:	In general this is true. However, if there is an obvious "red-flag" that you believe will negatively affect your candidacy, it may be to your advantage to bring it up—if you can address the matter in a way that should overcome the employer's fear. A candidate who is much older than the norm for people applying for a particular type of job may realize age is likely to be perceived as a negative by the employer. However, because of legal concerns, the interviewer may not feel free to mention it. If the applicant can make a good case for being hired over the more youthful applicants and allay the employer's apprehension, it will probably be to his or her advantage to raise the issue.

MYTH #16:	**If the interviewer asks about my weaknesses, I should indicate I have none.**
REALITY:	This response is likely to convey to the interviewer that you are less than honest, not an open communicator, or mildly delusional. Select a weakness that the

interviewer already knows about, one that has no relationship to the job, or one that you have improved upon.

MYTH #17:   **If there is something about me that may be perceived as negative, such as that I was fired from a job, I should fully explain the situation if asked about it.**

REALITY: Be honest in a way that reflects positively on you. Address the situation in a way that shows you have taken something positive from the experience—turned it into an opportunity. Keep your comments focused and brief. Don't dwell on what happened. This is a situation where most people talk too much. And don't disparage your former boss or company.

MYTH #18:   **If I am asked a clearly illegal question, I should set the interviewer straight so he or she won't do it again.**

REALITY: It may make you feel good for the moment, but it will rarely, if ever, get you the job. You might turn it around and politely indicate that it is a question you have never been asked before and you are curious as to why it is important to the job under consideration. But in most cases, if you still want an opportunity at the job, you will frame a positive response.

MYTH #19:   **It is best that I memorize responses to questions I expect to be asked.**

REALITY: You should anticipate questions and strategize the jist of your response. Do not try to memorize your response. At best it will sound rehearsed, and at worst you will suffer a lapse of memory in the midst of your answer. You should not be concerned about the exact words you use as you respond, but rather that you follow the jist of the message you planned in response to this question.

MYTH #20: I certainly don't want the employer to think I am desperate for a job, so I will be as low-key as possible.

REALITY: No, you do not want to appear desperate for just any job. But you do want to appear interested and enthusiastic about this job. Employers favor dynamic and energetic people who indicate genuine interest and enthusiasm with their work.

MYTH #21: I should not ask any questions until the end of the interview.

REALITY: You must validate the functional responsibilities of the position early in the interview if you are to be successful at projecting your qualifications and fit for the position.

MYTH #22: I will just answer the interviewer's questions. I don't want to ask any questions or he/she will think I haven't done my homework and researched the company.

REALITY: Certainly you need to prepare by researching the organization where you will interview. You do not want to ask basic questions which some basic data gathering should have answered. However, thoughtful and thorough research should also raise questions that go beyond basics. Employers indicate that the quality of the questions the interviewees ask can be as great a determinant of a job offer as the manner in which questions were answered.

MYTH #23: If I am asked about my salary expectations, I'll give a high figure. That way they will assume I am worth a lot.

REALITY: Try to avoid discussion of salary until there is a job offer on the table. Even then, try to get the interviewer to state a figure first. If you are in a situation where you are forced to respond, state a range based on salary comparables for the position which you gathered in preparation for the interview. The low figure (of the salary range) should not be

Try to avoid discussion of salary until there is a job offer on the table.

lower than the lowest figure you are willing to accept.

MYTH #24:   If I don't get a job offer at the end of my first interview with a company, I haven't done something right.

REALITY: Many job offers aren't extended until after several interviews have taken place. Except for entry-level jobs, most job seekers should expect more than one interview.

MYTH #25:   When they do offer me the job, the employer will want an acceptance right then and there.

REALITY: Perhaps the employer would like an immediate acceptance, but unless you are interviewing for an hourly position the employer won't expect one. Ask for at least 24 or 48 hours to consider the offer—longer if acceptance entails a long-distance move. Use the time to carefully consider the offer as well as check on the status of your candidacy with any other employers with whom you have been interviewing.

MYTH #26:   Once the interview is completed, I should thank the interviewer and go home and wait to hear from him or her.

REALITY: There are things you should do both before you leave the interview and once you get home. Before you leave the interview, ask what the next step is and the time frame. Will they be calling back candidates for additional interviews in the next week? Will they be making a hiring decision within the next ten days? Find out. Then ask if you may call to check on your status

> *Before you leave the interview, ask what the next step is and the time frame.*

if you haven't heard from them by that date. When the date rolls around, make that follow-up call. If you are now out of the running, you need to know so you can re-double your efforts elsewhere. If no decision has been made your call may add to their favorable impression of you—you demonstrate that you follow-through. You may even take this opportunity to briefly summarize again your great fit for the job and your interest in it.

The same day as the interview, write a letter thanking the employer for the opportunity to interview and a summary of how your skills and accomplishments can best meet the employer's needs. This is a business letter and should be typed or word processed on business stationery.

4

TYPES OF INTERVIEWS

J ob seekers who are unprepared may assume there is only one type of interview and one interview format. It is to your advantage to recognize and be prepared for different interview encounters. For in the end, each type of interview plays an important role in your job search.

TWO DIFFERENT TYPES OF INTERVIEWS

At Bernard Haldane Associates, we prepare our clients for two different types of interviews: referral and job. The **referral interview** is usually initiated by the job seeker who is actively involved in a networking campaign; this interview primarily focuses on acquiring information, advice, and referrals and is aimed at key decision-makers. The **job interview** is initiated by the employer and primarily focuses on screening candidates for a job offer.

While most job seekers only focus on preparing for the job interview, Bernard Haldane Associates know the importance of referral interviews and their clients actively seek them as part of their proactive job search campaign. Indeed, the referral interview often plays a key role in landing the perfect job. Neglect the referral interview and you may miss out on some of the most important job opportunities of a lifetime! As our clients remind us again and again, it's often the referral interview that resulted in by-passing the competition and landing the job.

INTERVIEWERS AND INTERVIEWEES

Many interviewers are seasoned professionals who are well prepared to conduct each interview. Most Human Resource personnel you encounter will probably fit this description. You may however, encounter an interviewer who conducts interviews infrequently, seems uncomfortable in that role or perhaps seems unprepared for your particular interview. A line manager, who interviews infrequently, might fall into the second category.

The two most important things are that you ask questions to gain the information you need and that you convey information to the interviewer that emphasizes your accomplishments. You must convey that you can do the job and that you are a good fit for the position. Unless, of course, you and the job are a misfit. If you are certain there is not a good fit, share this with the interviewer and ask to be referred on to someone who might have need of your skills. But be careful about ending your relationship with the interviewer prematurely. Perhaps you are not a good fit for this job, but as you engage the interviewer and focus on your strengths and accomplishments, he/she might be so impressed he will find another position for you within the firm where you are interviewing. It has happened to many Haldane clients.

> *Neglect the referral interview and you may miss out on some of the most important job opportunities of a lifetime!*

REFERRAL INTERVIEWS

Referral interviews are not the same as job interviews. You, the job applicant, ask for, set up, and conduct referral interviews as part of your networking activities. Often overlooked by job seekers, referral interviews are an important step toward the ultimate goal of landing a job. Once you have identified your success factors and have a targeted job objective, you should talk with people who work in your area of interest.

You have five basic goals in a referral interview:

- establish rapport
- get information
- get advice and reaction to how you are conducting your job search

- extend your network of contacts
- be remembered favorably and actively by those you interview

The value of referral interviews cannot be overstated because these interviews will impact on every other aspect of your job search. Someone with whom you conducted a referral interview may hear of a job opening that fits your accomplishments and your goals. He or she passes your name on to the hiring manager who calls you for an interview and you are later offered the job. You conduct a referral interview with a firm that has no openings in your line of work at that time, but later the interviewer remembers you when a vacancy occurs and you are called in, interviewed, and eventually offered the position. During your informational interviews you ask about salary ranges for the position you are targeting. Later, when offered your targeted position at another firm, you use the salary information you gathered during referral interviews to negotiate a higher salary than the employer initially offered.

Conducting referral interviews can be one of the most powerful job search strategies you employ. Sometimes referred to as informational or networking interviews, because they offer an opportunity to gain so much information useful to your job search, they often result in referrals as well. Your goal is not to get a job with these people—

> *The key to referral interviews is to never ask for a job. Ask instead for information, advice and referrals.*

only useful information, advice, and contacts for more information, advice, and referrals. The key to referral interviews is to never ask for a job. Ask instead for information, advice and referrals. Chapter 5 will focus on referral interviews.

JOB INTERVIEWS

Expect to encounter several types of job interviews. Most job seekers will experience some combination of these six types of job interviews:

- Screening
- One-on-one

- Sequential
- Series
- Panel
- Group

Questioning techniques within each of these interviews can run the gamut—from standard questions about your education, work history, and personality to behavior-based questions which attempt to probe your capabilities to make decisions, handle people, solve problems, and take important initiatives in the future. Some employers also like to ask stress questions. In the end, all of these interviews and questions are aimed at determining whether or not you are a good "fit" for the organization.

SCREENING INTERVIEWS

The screening interview may be the first of several job interviews you have with an employer. Whereas the referral interview is sought and conducted by you, the interviewee, the various job interviews—every interview other than the referral interview—are scheduled and conducted by the employer. The purpose of a screening interview, as the term implies, is to screen people in or out of further consideration.

Employers choose to use screening interviews because they save time and money. They save time because they can be conducted more quickly than other types of job interviews. Since they only attempt to decide whether a candidate is worth the time of a full interview, marginal candidates can be dispensed with more quickly. Screening interviews are less costly in part because they take less time and time is money. Screening interviews are especially frugal interviews to conduct when several of the candidates are from out of town. Rather than bring in ten candidates, if the employer can narrow the list to three by conducting screening interviews by telephone, both time and money have been saved.

Although screening interviews can be conducted face-to-face, especially in the case of job fairs, most screening interviews are conducted by telephone. If you receive a telephone call from an employer—no matter what the ostensible reason for the call, assume that you are being screened and take this call as seriously as you would any job interview.

What you say and how you say it will probably determine whether you will be invited to further interviews.

While you may know the importance of screening interviews, you do not know when they may occur. So it behooves you to always be prepared. By every telephone in your house and in a desk drawer or in your briefcase at the office you should be prepared for such an interview with a folder of key materials for quick reference. At the minimum you should have the following:

- paper and pen to jot down information
- scheduling calendar that is up-to-date with your previous commitments noted
- copy of your resume
- summary list of every company where you have sent your resume—with individual's names noted where possible
- listing of your statements of effectiveness—categorized and each statement repeated under every applicable category
- generic list of questions you might want to ask of the employer

These items are basic. You may wish to add additional items specific to your situation. When that screening phone call comes, you will be prepared. Most important of all, you'll sound confident and competent—important characteristics for "passing" the screening interview.

If a call comes from an employer at an awkward time—you have water boiling over on the range or your boss is standing over your shoulder at the office—simply ask the caller if you may call them back in ten minutes—or whatever timeframe is appropriate. There is no need to tell the caller why you can't take the call right now. Be sure to get the name of the caller, and get it right, as well as the telephone number. Take care of the water boiling on the range or get rid of your boss, get your materials together, look over any information you have on the employer who phoned, take a deep breath, smile, and return the call. In some ways you may be at an advantage asking to return the call. It will give you a chance to review your information on the employer and focus on the exchange that is about to take place.

> *Studies in communication indicate that much of our message is communicated nonverbally—as much as 90% by some estimates.*

Studies in communication indicate that much of our message is communicated nonverbally—as much as 90% by some estimates. This is divided between visual aspects, which will not be available in most telephone interviews, and paralanguage—the vocal cues. The most important thing your voice can convey is your enthusiasm. Keep an appropriate level of dynamism in your delivery!

ONE-ON-ONE INTERVIEWS

Face-to-face, one-on-one interviews are the most common type you will encounter. The applicant and the employer meet, usually at the company offices, to discuss the position and the candidate's skills, knowledge, and abilities—in other words the "fit" between you and the job opening. While a screening interview is likely to be conducted by someone in human resources, subsequent interviews are more likely, though not necessarily, conducted by someone from the department where the position is open. This person may be a department manager for lower and mid-level jobs and someone from upper-management—perhaps a vice president—for high level positions. If the interview is conducted by someone from the department with the open position, you can expect the interviewer to ask many specific job-related questions. If the interviewer is from human resources, the questions may be more general.

SEQUENTIAL INTERVIEWS

For many positions—especially those beyond entry-level—there will be more than one job interview. Multiple interviews are the rule, rather than the exception, for higher level positions. In fact, one Haldane client was interviewed 14 times by the same company before he was hired! Sequential interviews are simply a series of interviews with a decision being made either to screen the candidate in or out of further consideration after each interview. The candidates who make the cut are called back for another interview. Although each interview is frequently a one-on-one interview, the candidate could meet with more than one representative of the company at the same time. The candidate could meet with different interviewers in subsequent interviews or meet with the same person who conducted the previous interview. Usually if there are several interviews, the applicant will meet additional persons from the organization rather than just the same person over and over again. However, the previous interviewer may be part of a future mix of individuals.

When sequential interviews are planned, the first interview(s) will usually deal with job issues—the fit between the applicant and the open position. Terms of employment, such as salary and benefits will not likely be discussed, and certainly not in depth, until an offer is, or is about to be made. This can work to your advantage as you have additional opportunities to value the position as well as opportunities to share your accomplishments with the employer.

SERIES INTERVIEWS

Like sequential interviews, serial interviews consist of several interviews. But whereas a decision was made after each of the interviews in the sequential interview process as to whether a candidate would be called back for another interview, serial interviews are set up as a series from the beginning and no decision is made concerning the candidate until the entire series of interviews has been completed.

Usually the interviews are scheduled with a variety of people. They may consist of several types of interviews and be held over one or several days. A candidate may meet with a vice-president of the company early in the day and then have a series of meetings with a couple of department managers during the morning. A lunch meeting may be scheduled with additional managers, after which the candidate may return to meet one-on-one with a series of additional people. The evening may be free or may continue with dinner at a nearby restaurant or in someone's home. The next day may bring additional interviews or an opportunity for the candidate to demonstrate his or her skill in some way. A candidate interviewing for a faculty position may be asked to teach a class, an advertising executive may be asked to present part of an advertising campaign, or a salesperson may be asked to sell a product.

If you find yourself engaged in a series of interviews, make sure to treat each interview with each different person as if it were your first.

After talking all day with a series of individuals, some candidates become mentally fatigued and don't focus as well on their accomplishments or their dynamism wanes. Remember this is your first interview with this individual. Remain focused on getting the information about the position that you will need to sell yourself and later to make your decision when you are offered the job. Be sure to answer questions fully—even though this is the third time you've been asked that question in the same day. Continue to sell your strengths and maintain your dynamic presentation as you respond.

> *If you find yourself engaged in a series of interviews, make sure to treat each interview with each different person as if it were your first.*

PANEL INTERVIEWS

Panel interviews occur infrequently—less frequently these days than they once did. But you need to be aware of them since it is possible you may encounter one. In a panel interview, you are interviewed by several people at one time. Whether intended or not, the panel interview produces greater stress for the job candidate. After all, you have more people to analyze and respond to simultaneously which puts you in an inherently reactive situation. Some panel interviews are intended to put pressure on the applicant—part of what the employer wants to discover is how well the interviewee maintains composure under stress.

If you find yourself the center of a panel interview, take a deep breath and try to remain calm. Take each question one by one, ask for clarification if the intent of the question is not clear or the scope extremely broad. Ask for the opportunity to respond to the important question posed by one interviewer before being pushed into a response to a question by another one of the panel members. Chances are the content of your answers is less important in this situation than your ability to remain unflustered in the face of stress.

GROUP INTERVIEWS

While an uncommon interview type for most positions, group interviews do take place. They may be most likely conducted for jobs in education and counseling. If you find yourself being interviewed along with several other applicants for the same or a similar position, you are in a group interview. We are aware of instances where a group interview is conducted as a screening interview to winnow the number of applicants for jobs where the applicant pool is very large—such as for flight attendants for airlines. A group interview is sometimes used in the later stages of job interviews because the employer trys to gain data not thought available in a one-on-one setting.

In group interviews the employer wants to observe first-hand how applicants interact with one another. The interpersonal skills and personality traits that surface can speak volumes about how the candidate may interact on the job as a manager, with colleagues, or with clients. Often a question will be posed to the group or the group will be given a problem to solve. If the applicants exhibit positive leadership behaviors in the group setting, employers tend to think they will take charge and be a leader in the workplace. If a candidate seeks to draw other people into the discussion and attempts to build consensus, and keeps the group focused on the task at hand, the inference is the candidate will behave in a similar manner in working for the firm.

In group interviews, the content of the discussion is usually of secondary importance. Of more importance to the employer is the behavior taking place. This is behavior-based interviewing at its most basic level!

5

THE REFERRAL INTERVIEW

For more than 50 years, Bernard Haldane Associates has pioneered one of the most effective job search techniques for getting job interviews and offers—the referral interview. Known in some job search circles as networking and informational interviews, this technique has proven successful for thousands of our clients. Indeed, many of our clients identify the referral interview as the single most important technique they used in getting a job. Without the referral interview, their job search would have taken a different path and perhaps resulted in a less than satisfactory outcome. A sometimes controversial technique, nonetheless, it works to the benefit of both the job seeker and employer. When done properly, it is the most powerful job search technique you can use for both shortening your job search time and landing a job that is right for you.

THE HALDANE NETWORKING APPROACH

The Haldane networking approach is designed to create a set of contacts that generates both information and support. It links you with people who can help you now and whom you can help later. The network can begin with people you know, such as friends, relatives, and professional associates. You can then expand your network to include individuals in your specific career area whom you don't know at present. A well organized networking campaign will result in building a large network of individuals, many of whom will literally become your eyes and ears for information, advice, and job leads. Rather than get a job by responding to a formal job announcement (classified ad or Internet posting), you'll land a job through your personal networking activities—perhaps before a job is ever announced. Your networking activities result in numerous referral interviews that lead to job interviews and offers.

Networking and referral interviews are somewhat controversial job search methods. Many people believe that decision makers are too busy to meet with job seekers and they have little interest in being helpful. They also believe requesting advice and information is "using" others for selfish reasons. These beliefs are false and are developed in our formative years by a culture that tends to demand we "stand on our own two feet." Some individuals even consider a request for assistance as a weakness. While you may feel that way initially, as you gather information and build your network, you will have opportunities, in turn, to be helpful to those you interview. The reality is that our society has become more sophisticated, complex, and competitive, to the extent that it is virtually impossible for anyone to live and work effectively without the help and support of others. It is, therefore, imperative that we seek help from others as we need it, and at the same time, be willing to give help to others as they need it. Over time, your network will become a much needed tool that allows you to gain invaluable support and information. It also allows you to return that support via people who will approach you in your new position.

> **Client Feedback**
>
> *"The most important interviews were referrals that I scheduled myself. With the exception of one interview, every referral interview with company personnel offered me a position. I feel that the personal contacts in conjunction with my resume, presented a total package for the interviewer. This definitely made a difference."*
>
> —L.M.

FOCUS ON DECISION MAKERS

When networking in your career field, target only people in the company who have the power to hire and create positions. These people are called "decision makers" and can be in any level of the company. Consider for a moment the typical business manager. At almost any time, he/she has some problem which probably can only be resolved by replacing or adding an employee. Since replacing or finding a new em-

> *When networking in your career field, target only people in the company who have the power to hire and create positions.*

ployee is time consuming and costly, it's the kind of problem the manager will often postpone. Instead, the manager will solve other more immediate and easily resolved problems. Often these personnel problems are not shared with others. Only the manager is aware of future staff needs or of dissatisfaction with a staff member.

Therefore, whenever you have an opportunity to meet privately with a "decision maker" to discuss a job function or a particular career path, it is likely that your discussion will stimulate reflection on immediate and future needs. You have no way of knowing whether an executive has plans for staff changes or additions. But you can be reasonably certain your discussions will cause the executive to evaluate you in the light of organizational needs.

Meetings with decision makers, therefore, represent the greatest possible resource for positions that can, and probably will, be filled without any real competition from others. Further, these meetings allow you to avoid the highly competitive and frustrating avenues provided by newspaper advertisements, Internet job searching, and employment agencies.

REFERRAL INTERVIEWS

The job market is not an impersonal conglomerate of machines and statistics, but a vast network of interrelating human beings. How quickly and efficiently you find the right position and move ahead in your career is directly proportional to your understanding and application of certain basic principles of human nature. Here are four which are fundamental to a productive marketing campaign:

1. People like to say "yes;" they dislike being put into the negative position of rejecting you.

2. People like and need honest recognition.

3. People like to give advice; asking a person's advice is granting that person recognition.

4. People prefer to be approached gradually; they dislike being put under pressure.

The most important tool for navigating in this vast people network is built upon these very points. We call it a **referral interview**. You are in a referral interview whenever you are not being interviewed for a specific job. The referral interview is a purposeful discussion with another person about your career. Thus, it is very different from the job interview. It is an excellent way to obtain information and to make contacts and, when implemented correctly, will lead to job interviews. Your understanding of the purpose and technique of the referral approach is going to be one of the most important tools of your job search.

The experiences of thousands of job seekers and the results of numerous national research projects have shown that very often the quickest way to get a job is never to ask for one. That's right. Never ask for a job when you are on a referral interview. First, it is unlikely that when you ask a person for a job, there will be just such a job open at that time, or that interviewers will know where such a job opening exists. So, chances are that you will get a negative answer. Secondly, when you ask for

> ## Client Feedback
>
> *"There is no doubt that your referral interview process works very well. All the homework, discussions, and training were necessary steps to successful interviews. People are willing to help in promoting careers and recommending other individuals to talk to. I am quite certain that I would not be where I am today without having gone through all your procedures. The idea of becoming a real estate appraiser came from several people I had never met before, and would probably not have met had I not gone through your training process."*
>
> —K.B.

a job, you are almost always putting the individual in a negative posture of saying "no" or turning you down. This will make the interviewer uncomfortable, and the more uncomfortable another person feels, the quicker that person will want to forget you. This is just the opposite of what you are trying to achieve.

Case In Point

With a Ph.D. in Forest Ecology, T.H. was interested in speaking to the V.P. at Timberworld Corp. in charge of all forest lands west of the Rockies. Everyone told him that he would never be able to get through to him to set an appointment, but he sent an approach letter anyway.

On the stated day he called the V.P.'s office whereupon the secretary patched him through to his cell phone. He was able to set an appointment on the spot.

You are certainly not trying to hide the fact that you are looking for a position. In fact, you are on a very active marketing campaign with the specific purpose of finding the right position, and it is important that this is absolutely clear. However, you are only being realistic when you assume that individuals will not have, or know of, an opening at the exact time you are talking with them. When you ask for a job, you put individuals under pressure. When you make it clear that you do not expect them to have a job opening, or to know of one, you take the pressure off them; they become more willing to listen to you and to remember you favorably.

The referral interview is closely akin to a business meeting. Since you've called the meeting, you must provide the agenda. Likewise, it is incumbent upon you to define the parameters, expectations, and goals; facilitate the process toward your objective; and conclude with either a specific next step or a well-defined end.

You should also consider the referral interview as a process. Though there are specific stages that all referral interviews pass through, each individual interview should be geared to the particular person you are speaking with. Remember, unlike a job interview, in a referral interview, *you are the interviewer* and the person to whom you are speaking is the interviewee. As such, each referral interview—as each individual baseball game—should be subtly and acutely different from all those that come before and all those that are to follow.

As noted previously in Chapter 4, in contrast to a job interview, a referral interview has five specific purposes:

1. Establish rapport.
2. Get information.
3. Acquire advice and reaction to product, market, fit.
4. Extend your contact network.
5. Be remembered favorably and actively.

Establish Rapport

In establishing rapport, you need to get to know the people you are interviewing. Let them know who you are and be certain they see you and your objective clearly. The best way to establish personal contact with individuals is to take a genuine interest in them. In any encounter with another person, your attitude will be reflected to you by that person. It is not an issue of techniques, but of genuine, constructive attitudes.

Get Information

Think of the interviewee as a person with whom you are establishing a professional relationship. This is a very different view from the commonly held assumption that a "contact" is a person who can pull strings for you, who can give you a job, or who can find one for you. Employees must be seen as sources of information. Most specifically, you are seeking information about your job market. The more information you can accumulate, the more knowledge you will have. Knowledge is power. The more you have, the more easily you will navigate in the job market. Such information might include the latest developments in your field of interest, focusing on individuals, articles, and publications; problem areas in different parts of the market; professional associations; or salary ranges for particular positions in your geographic region. If you come out of your interview with more information than you went in with, you have had a successful referral interview.

Acquire Advice and Reaction to Product, Market, Fit

You need advice on, and reaction to, the way you conduct your marketing campaign. Job seeking is an area in which there are few experts. Comments and suggestions regarding your approach and presentation will help you improve your interviewing effectiveness. Remem-

12 RULES OF NETWORKING

Networking opportunities are everywhere. To capitalize on these opportunities, the following networking tips should assist you in your job search:

- When, at a group activity, meet as many people as you can. Don't sit with the same people you came with. Introduce yourself to new people. Include all ages, genders, and cultures.

- Exchange business cards. Explain what you do.

- Wear a name tag, include your business, and a line to stimulate interest. Example: *We do the impossible and the unique!*

- Act like a host, not a guest. Introduce yourself. Help others make connections also.

- Save business for later. Don't do business with networking.

- Keep moving. Don't talk to any one person for too long; make an appointment or move on.

- Be proactive. Don't wait for others to suggest what they might do for you; look for ways to help them.

- Follow-up. Write notes or call back. Set appointments to meet.

- Avoid too much small talk; time is valuable. Explore how you can support each other.

- Set a goal. Try to meet at least five new people. Try to find one person with whom you can set an appointment.

- Look for ways to help others. Introduce new friends to people you think they should know.

- Keep the contact. Call back just to stay in touch and up-to-date. Send a thank you note, or some piece of information you think may be of interest, whenever you can.

ber, when you are sincere in asking for advice, you acknowledge the other person's expertise. Such recognition is generally well received and will prompt the individual to want to help you.

Extend Your Contact Network

You continue building your contact network when you ask for one or more referrals. The person you are talking with is now part of your personal contact network. When interviewees have understood who you are, what you can do, and where you are going, they will want to help you get there. In almost every case, you will come out of the interview with the names of one or more people to contact. An exception may be when an interviewee wants to consider you for a position within the organization.

Be Remembered Favorably and Actively

Ask for permission to keep the interviewee informed about your progress. This will not only be given; it will be appreciated. Every interviewee, having become part your contact network, now has a stake in your success. Everyone feels good about contributing to someone else's achievement. In the course of time, other thoughts and ideas will come to those you have interviewed that they will want to share with you, provided you have established positive rapport with them. If you have accomplished the other four purposes, you will have little difficulty being remembered favorably; but just to make sure, you will write a thank-you letter within 24 hours after the interview.

When you have had some practice, you will discover that the referral approach will put you far ahead of most other job seekers. You will have interviews with people you never expected to contact. Your job search will progress in relation to the effectiveness of your referral interviews.

INFORMATIONAL AND REFERRAL MEETINGS

Information and referral meetings are the two primary vehicles you will use in your marketing campaign. They provide a method of career exploration and a way of discovering jobs that are not publicly advertised. Indeed, it is estimated that up to 75% of all jobs are not publicly advertised. Through informational and referral meetings, you will be

Case In Point

Tanya came to us as a very scared, recent college graduate. Her grades were ok but not great considering her major was pre-med.

She decided that she would like to move to Boston and look for a Public Relations job. We identified the PR firms in Boston and she began sending referral letters out. Tanya went to Boston and had a number of very productive referral and job interviews.

Tanya had always been interested in Tiffany's, and discovered that she had a friend who knew someone there. Tanya was able, through her friend, to secure a referral interview at Tiffany's. The conversation turned to a part-time opening that Tiffany's had. Within a few meetings, Tanya was able to turn the part-time opening into a full-time, salary with benefits position paying $32,000 per year! Not bad for a brand new college graduate.

able to break into this "hidden job market" which has a wealth of career positions and very little competition.

Let's start by defining this interviewing technique. Informational meetings take on two distinct forms: the "direct contact" informational meeting and the referral meeting. An informational meeting is with someone you do not know. The individual's name will probably come from your research through a corporate report, advertisement, newspaper article, reference book, or the Internet.

Conversely, the referral meeting is with someone you know, or someone you have previously met has recommended him or her to you. Both of you have a mutual acquaintance and possibly something in common. The techniques used in conducting referral meetings are identical to those used in informational meetings. Remember, informational and referral meetings are not job interviews.

The basic rule of thumb is this: "If you are not on a job interview for a specific position, then you are in an informational meeting." If you confuse these interviews with job interviews, your approach makes your interviewee uncomfortable—you're asking for a job rather than requesting information, advice, and referrals.

In order to effectively put the referral approach into practice, you need to go through five steps or phases:

1. Develop contact and target lists.
2. Write approach letters.
3. Make follow-up calls.
4. Conduct referral interviews.
5. Send thank-you letters and follow-up.

Develop Contact and Target Lists

You should begin the networking process by developing two important lists for initiating the informational and referral meetings:

1. People you already know who can function as primary contacts for advice and information. This list should include at least 25 people but may include over 100 names.
2. Industries and companies you wish to target. Identify at least ten companies you are interested in investigating.

Start by listing individuals, industries, and companies who you know that might be able to give you information and advice:

Primary Contacts For Advice and Information
(People I Know)

Former Employers

_____

_____

_____

Bankers/Financial Consultants

_____

_____

_____

Accountants

_____

_____

_____

Lawyers

_____

_____

_____

Business Executives/Owners

_____

_____

_____

Past Business Associates

_____

_____

_____

Clergy

_____

_____

_____

Political/Civic Leaders

_____

_____

_____

College Professors, Deans, and Presidents

_____

_____

_____

College Alumni

_____

_____

_____

Sales People

_____

_____

_____

Doctors, Dentists, etc.

_____

_____

_____

Business Consultants

_____

_____

_____

Financial Planners, Real Estate Professionals

_____

_____

_____

Friends, Relatives

_____

_____

_____

Associations

_____

_____

_____

Professional Organizations

_____

_____

_____

Others

_____

_____

_____

_____

_____

List of Target Companies

Prepare a list of target companies in which you would seek possible employment. To acquire information on a particular company of interest, ask for a corporate annual report or other literature from the company and do library research with periodicals, newspapers, publications, Internet, etc. Compile basic information on each company as follows:

Company: _____
Industry: _____
Executive Contact: _____ Phone: (___) ___ -_____
Address: _____
Notes: _____

Company: _____
Industry: _____
Executive Contact: _____ Phone: (___) ___ -_____
Address: _____
Notes: _____

Company: _____
Industry: _____
Executive Contact: _____ Phone: (___) ___ -_____
Address: _____
Notes: _____

Company: _____
Industry: _____
Executive Contact: _____ Phone: (___) ___ -_____
Address: _____
Notes: _____

Company: _____
Industry: _____
Executive Contact: _____ Phone: (___) ___ -_____
Address: _____
Notes: _____

Company: _____

Industry: _____

Executive Contact: _____   Phone: (___)___ -_____

Address: _____

Notes: _____

Company: _____

Industry: _____

Executive Contact: _____   Phone: (___)___ -_____

Address: _____

Notes: _____

Company: _____

Industry: _____

Executive Contact: _____   Phone: (___)___ -_____

Address: _____

Notes: _____

Company: _____

Industry: _____

Executive Contact: _____   Phone: (___)___ -_____

Address: _____

Notes: _____

Write Approach Letters

Plan to write two types of letters in your networking campaign: the direct contact letter and the referral letter.

- **Direct Contact Letter:** This letter is designed to get an informational interview with the decision maker in your field who will be able to assist you in your job search. The person you contact will NOT be known to you, nor will you have been "sent" to him or her by someone else (a referral).

- **Referral Letter:** This letter is identical to the direct contact letter except you have been "referred" to the decision maker. If you can get the attention of someone through a contact, you have gained a tremendous advantage and you are almost guaranteed an interview.

These letters may be the most important ones you write during your job search campaign. Their sole purpose is to obtain a meeting. They must be totally personal and unique—only you can write them. Each letter should be tailored to the specific situation for which it is used. However, the following format is common to all direct contact/referral letters.

1. Date, name, title, and address of the decision maker, and the salutation.

2. Open the letter with a warm personal statement, explaining why you chose this particular person (this paragraph will be different for each person you write.). For example, if you are writing to a person without a referral, you might say, "My research has identified you as a person with a strong perspective on the engineering and construction industry in this area." If the letter is the result of a referral, use a phrase like, "Ralph Wilson suggested I write to you..."

3. Explain your current situation and what you are attempting to do. Mention that you have enclosed a resume or professional profile only to give him or her a better understanding of your objective and to provide valuable feedback concerning the style and content of the professional profile. For example, "In making a career change into the computer systems industry, I feel I need the advice of leaders at your level." You may also tell the individual of a significant achievement of yours.

4. State that you are not expecting the person to know of a current opening but would appreciate his or her assistance, guidance, and opinion about what you are doing. State clearly what you see as the purpose of the interview. You are seeking his or her reaction to:

   ■ Your stated objective.
   ■ Your plans for marketing yourself.
   ■ Your presentation.
   ■ Market areas on which you wish to concentrate.

5. Tell him or her you recognize the value of his or her time and will call in a few days to schedule a brief twenty minute meeting. Never give a specific date or time that you will call. You may be sick, or out of town during the specific time you were to call and will lose your credibility.

6. Use an upbeat close, "Your information is very important to me and I really look forward to meeting with you."

This letter will be used for at least 80% of your approaches. You will need to draft several letters of this type until your style becomes natural as well as clear and purposeful. The sample letters on pages 52–54 incorporate these writing principles.

Send your letter to the targeted individual after you have confirmed that the person still works at that company, their title, and address. Confirmation is as easy as calling the company and telling the administrative assistant that you are sending a business letter (true) to the individual and want to make sure you have his or her title and name spelled directly. Complete this confirmation step even if you have been "referred" to the person. You may discover errors in the title and spelling of the name.

Make Follow-Up Calls

Make a follow-up call within two days after the letter arrives. The purpose of this call is to set an appointment. Have your appointment book, a copy of the letter you sent, a copy of your background summary, and your set of interview questions in front of you for reference. Always identify yourself before speaking. Speak in an enthusiastic manner and keep a list of the points you want to say in front of you. If you get thrown off track by an unexpected question or reaction, it is relatively easy to recover when you have your thoughts written out. Of course, they have to be adapted to meet individual situations, but in general plan to proceed as follows:

1. **Voicemail:** You will often get voicemail rather than the individual you're expecting to speak with. Talking to a machine causes some people to become nervous or flustered. To overcome this, simply hang up when you get the voicemail recording. You can then:

Direct Contact/Referral Letter

April 23, _____

Their Name
Title
Company
Address

Dear M:

FOR REFERRAL LETTER START HERE:

I recently had a conversation with (list the full name of your referral) and (s)he suggested that I should contact you directly, as someone who could be most helpful in providing information to support my career objective.

FOR A DIRECT CONTACT LETTER, START HERE:

The purpose of this letter is to ask for your help in making a career transition into your industry. As an established and respected member of the industry, your advice and counsel would be greatly appreciated.

TO COMPLETE EITHER LETTER, CONTINUE HERE:

As I am researching my career options, I do not expect you to have a position, nor do I assume that you may know of one. My purpose, however, is to request an opportunity to receive your professional and candid opinion of my experience and background as it relates to the industry. To this end, I would like to meet with you for about 20 minutes.

My experience entails (list your "Qualification" paragraph from your background summary here)...

My background summary is enclosed so that you will have more information about me before we meet.

Please anticipate a call in the next few days to arrange a meeting at a mutually convenient time. I look forward to meeting you.

Sincerely,

Your Name
Address
Phone Number
Email
Enclosure

Direct Contact Letter

April 23, _____

Mr. John Smith, President
Smith Financial Services
1415 Second Avenue
Seattle, WA 98101

Dear Mr. Smith:

I am writing to you because of your knowledge in the financial services field. As one of the leaders in the consulting field here in King County, you have both the experience and knowledge that will enable me to fully understand the financial services arena.

I (am about to leave the military service) or (have just left the military service) and am considering a career move into the financial planning profession. Before making a firm commitment, I need to gather as much information as possible from professionals like you to make an informed decision. Let me assure you, Mr. Smith, this is not a request for a job. I do not foresee you having a position open nor do I presume you will know of one. I would, however, sincerely appreciate your objective views and counsel on my experience, career goals, and how these may assist me in my career transition.

I have completed my Master's degree in Accounting and will take my CPA exam shortly. I have extensive experience in the business community dealing with budgets and fiscal matters as comptroller of various organizations that annually deal with over $11.8 million.

My background summary is enclosed so that you may review my achievements in advance. It will allow you to know me better before we meet and help you provide valuable feedback concerning the content of my summary. I will call you next week to arrange a brief 15-20 minute meeting at a mutually convenient time.

I look forward to meeting with you and learning more about the financial planning field.

Sincerely,

Your Name
Address
Phone Number
Email
Enclosure

Referral Letter

April 23, _____

Mr. Robert T. Whitworth
President
Whitworth Enterprises
1017 Pacific Avenue
Tacoma, WA 98531

Dear Mr. Whitworth:

Recently I had a conversation with Ms. Helen Thompson, the Vice President of Wilson, Thompson and Associates, about careers in computer graphics. Ms. Thompson urged me to contact you for valuable information and possible assistance in making my decision.

Let me assure you, as I did Ms. Thompson, I am not approaching you for a job, nor do I assume you will know of an opening. However, I would sincerely appreciate your objective views on my experience, my career objective, marketing approach, and how I can make a potential transition in the least amount of time.

Having just completed my Bachelor of Fine Arts degree with an emphasis in graphic arts and photography, I have current knowledge, but somewhat limited experience in computer graphics and some exposure to CAD and other computer-aided graphics programs.

My background summary is enclosed for your information and so that you may provide valuable feedback about my experience and achievements when we meet.

In the next few days, I will call to arrange a 15-20 minute meeting at a mutually convenient time. I look forward to meeting and talking with you.

Sincerely,

Your Name
Address
Phone Number
Email
Enclosure

- Prepare notes or a written script, practice it a few times, then call again. If using a script, guard against sounding as if you are reading.

- Speak naturally, relax, and breathe.

- Keep your message brief. Simply state your name, phone number, time, and date.

- Tell the individual that you are following-up on a letter you sent and will call at a later time or (s)he may return your call. You may want to give him or her a time to reach you. If you give the option of returning your call, relay the best time to reach you and allow several days for the person to call before you call again.

- Remember, your goal is to maintain control of your marketing campaign. Be responsible for all action items affecting your campaign.

The voicemail message and your response might go like this:

Voicemail: This is Ruth Anderson. I am not available to take your call. Please leave a message and I will return your call as soon as possible.

You: Ms. Anderson, this is William Montgomery. I am calling you regarding a letter you should have received in the last few days. I can be reached at (425) 462-7308 between 8 and 5 o'clock. I look forward to your call.

2. **Administrative Assistant:** If you are not put into voicemail, chances are you will be speaking with an administrative assistant. It is important to establish rapport with this person who is a facilitator and valuable business contact. When speaking, be firm and positive without being rude. If you seem hesitant, rude, pushy, or unsure of yourself, you may be put on the defensive, limiting your chances of getting to talk to the person you are calling. Always expect to get through to the executive.

Case In Point

One client sent letters to his first three primary contacts. He called the first one to schedule the meeting and the person said, "I don't do that sort of thing" and slammed the phone down. Nice friend. He then called the second person and got his wife, who said he was only going to be in town for about a half hour between planes. My client was getting a little frustrated, but he called the third person who did agree to meet with him. This person was fantastic, not only giving him lots of good information, but he then pulled out his rolodex and gave him 47 names! The client reported to me that now he knows how this is supposed to work.

If asked the nature of your call by the administrative assistant, say that you sent a letter and are following up on the correspondence; your call is expected. Ask to speak with the executive by name. If true, explain that Mr./Ms. X and VP of ABC Corporation suggested that you talk with the executive. Be pleasant but brief. Be assertive but not aggressive.

If the executive is out or otherwise unavailable, find out the best time to call back and then call back at that time! Retain the initiative. Do not wait to be called back. It is also advisable to get the administrative assistant's name, since you will be calling back and there may be more than one person answering the phone. Put his or her name on your copy of the letter you sent so this information is readily available. People like to hear their name!

The following phone conversation might take place between you and an administrative assistant once you learn the person you are called for is in a meeting or not in the office:

You: When is a good time to call back?

Assistant: She should be out of the meeting at 10am. She then has another meeting at 10:30am. I would call her between 10 and 10:15am.

| **You:** | Thanks Julie. (Use the name this individual has pro-vided—in many instances, it may only be a first name.) I'll call her then. I appreciate your help. Good-bye. |
| **Assistant:** | Bye. (*Make sure you call on time!*) |

3. **The Executive:** When you connect with the executive, do the following:

■ Identify yourself, state that you sent a letter, and restate the purpose of your proposed meeting.

■ Mention at least two specific dates and hours that are convenient for you to meet. (Have your appointment book available. Do not say, "I can meeting anytime." This makes you look disorganized or inactive.)

■ If the executive responds with a different date and time, take a few seconds before responding, even if you know that the time is clear. If you respond too quickly, you communicate that you have nothing else to do and are sitting around.

■ Check your calendar, then set the time, thank the execu-tive for the appointment, and then close the conversa-tion gracefully, thanking him or her for the time.

In case your letter has been misunderstood, approach the situation as follows:

■ Explain briefly what you are doing, that you are not ex-pecting the person you are calling to have a position avail-able, or even to know of one; however, you do need some important information and that you believe the interviewer would be the person best qualified to give it.

■ End by indicating your enthusiasm for the meeting. Re-member, you are trying to gain career information and counsel.

■ Try not to conduct an interview over the phone. Do your best to obtain a face-to-face meeting.

Effective Phone Techniques

Phone technique, a primary factor in a career search, is learned through continued practice with phone presentations and is very important in making a presentation become "second nature" to you. Technique, coupled with guidelines for a basic phone presentation, assures a smooth and effective delivery. Consider these aspects:

1. **VOICE:** Can almost by itself assure a successful presentation. When adjusting the voice to the telephone, you should speak directly into the mouthpiece. Test your volume with a tape recorder; set the volume so it comes over evenly and can be heard without straining.

2. **DICTION:** Is equally as important as the voice. The telephone isolates it, magnifies every imperfection, and distracts from the thought you wish to convey.

3. **VOCABULARY:** Adjust to the respondent's vocabulary level as nearly as possible. Be professional; never include any profane words in YOUR vocabulary no matter how slight, regardless of what language the respondent uses.

4. **SPEED OF CONVERSATION:** Adjust the speed of conversation: with a slow-speaking person, speak slightly faster to enhance concentration on what you are saying; with an extremely fast-speaking person, a shade slower is the key to accomplishing the best results.

5. **AUTHORITY AND SELF CONFIDENCE:** Develop a high degree of authority and self confidence in your voice. Secretaries will put you right through to the decision maker when the qualities in your voice demand it. Speak with conviction to demonstrate authority. The most guaranteed method to help you acquire authority and self confidence, however, is control of your presentation and positive thinking.

6. **ATTITUDE:** Be upbeat. It's a positive, friendly feeling that is easily transmitted. Place a mirror in front of you while dialing to make certain a positive attitude prevails.

7. **FIRMNESS:** *Never apologize.* Be courteous, considerate, and confident, but avoid making a direct apology. Do not open a conversation with a comment like, "I am sorry to have bothered you."

8. **PRACTICE:** Makes perfect. The top professionals in every field reached success through practicing their craft. Professional sports, for example, demand that even the best attend all practices. And in telephoning you, likewise, can be the best…practice, practice, practice.

In summary, apply a perfected phone technique with well thought out presentations and you WILL achieve the desired results.

■ Keep the conversation short, and indicate you are looking forward to meeting the executive personally. You will
most likely have to conduct some phone interviews,
which are better than none at all, but don't make it a
habit.

If your letter has not been received, read, or remembered, it is advisable, in most cases, to offer to call back within the next couple of
days after the individual has had a chance to read it. If the letter has not
been received, send a copy of your letter and follow through as before.

The following script has worked well for our clients:

Assistant:	SoundTech Systems, Julie speaking. How may I help you?
You:	Hello Julie. Is Ms. Anderson in?
Assistant:	Yes she is. Who may I say is calling?
You:	My name is William Montgomery.
Assistant:	Just a moment.
Executive:	Ruth Anderson. How can I help you?
You:	Hello, Ms. Anderson. I recently sent you a letter con-cerning information I'm seeking about the electronics field. Have you received it?
Executive:	Yes I have. Just a minute…I've got it right here. How can I help you?
You:	As my letter outlines, I am researching the electronics industry as a possible career field and am talking with executives like you to find out if this is an area I should pursue. I recently left the service and I don't want to make any career decisions without gaining as much in-formation as I can. I would like to ask you for advice and counsel about opportunities and would like to meet with you for about 15-20 minutes at a mutually conve-nient time. Would next Tuesday afternoon or Thursday morning be possible?
Executive:	Are you looking for a job? We don't have any openings at this time.

You:	(Yes, I am looking for a position.) (No, I haven't launched my search yet.) Even so, as my letter indicated, I am not going to ask you for one, nor will I expect you'll know of any openings. I am merely asking for your candid and professional advice as to how my experience relates to the industry. I consider you a valuable resource for my future. Only experts such as you can tell me if I have the qualifications to succeed in the industry.
Executive:	I'm not sure if I can help, but . . . next Tuesday afternoon at 2:30pm is currently open. How does that sound?
You:	(*After a few seconds delay*) That sounds fine. I will be at your office on Tuesday afternoon, the 22nd, at 2:30pm. I really appreciate you taking the time to assist me. I look forward to seeing you.
Executive:	Great, Tuesday afternoon. See you then. Bye.
You:	Good-bye.

Conduct Referral Interviews

Once you get to the stage of the actual referral interview, preparation for this interview is essential. Before you go on the interview, think through very carefully what your purpose is in seeing this person. Be sure you understand exactly what you want to accomplish in the meeting and the specific information you hope to elicit. Keep in mind any constraints that may affect the interview. Be particularly sensitive to time issues. Prepare a list of questions appropriate for this particular interview. Again, since you have requested the meeting, it is your responsibility to plan a meaningful agenda. Unless you convey a definite purpose through the questions you ask, you will lose control of the interview and make it difficult, if not impossible, for the interviewees to help you. Keep in mind the following five goals of such an interview:

1. **Establish goodwill and understanding.** Get to know who the interviewees are by asking realistic and honest questions about them and how they got to where they are today. Let them know who you are and what you are trying to do. Be certain they clearly see your career objective. Take genuine

interest in them as a person. After all, they are the experts and you are trying to learn from them.

2. **Provide and collect information.** You are establishing a professional relationship with these executives. Show how they can assist you in your goals and ask for their professional perspective on your goals in the field you are discussing. Knowledge is strength, but the application of knowledge is power. The more knowledge you have, the more potential power you have when you apply the knowledge. Ask very specific questions about the industry, the market, challenges in the next few years, the strength and weakness of the industry, etc.

3. **Receive advice and counsel.** Comments and suggestions regarding your approach and presentation will help you improve your interviewing effectiveness. Let them know their professional opinion is crucial to your success. What can you do to make the transition from one career field to another quickly, benefiting both you and an employer?

> **Case In Point**
>
> *One of our clients, who was in senior operations management with a local retail chain, had a breakfast meeting with a President of a local department store chain. The two of them had never met before. After spending time with the President, the President offered to write twenty letters of introduction for my client to twenty Presidents of local companies. In the end, my client obtained a position with one of these contacts as the Vice President of Operations for a start-up children's activity outlet.*

4. **Extend your network.** Unless the interviewee is considering you for a possible position, you will generally get a name or two of people who can provide additional information and guidance. Ask if there are any other people in the field

who might be able to provide vital information as the executive sitting across from you has done.

5. **Be remembered professionally and favorably.** Ask if you can keep them abreast of your progress and if you can contact them in the future to verify information or to answer questions. The answer will be virtually 100% "yes." The executives have an interest in your success and they are part of your network. They like being the "good guys." Because you have done your homework, presented yourself professionally, and established a positive rapport, you will have little difficulty being remembered in the most positive light.

Once you are at the meeting, you should begin by thanking the individual for taking time to meet with you. Explain the purpose of your visit and recap your letter's purpose. Reassure the person that you do not expect him or her to find or give you a job. After stating your purpose, you might, for example, say something like this:

"I am currently researching alternatives in which I can use my leadership and technical trouble-shooting skills. In my recent conversation with John Jones, he spoke very highly of you and suggested that you, as a successful manufacturing manager, would be an excellent source of information."

Since the referral interview is a meeting to gather information and advice relevant to your marketing campaign and your career, the logical starting point is a discussion of your job objective and your areas of strength. Most interviewees will want to know about your background as well as your objective. Use the accomplishments mentioned on your resume to illustrate your areas of strength. Unless the interviewee sees clearly who you are and where you are going, it will be extremely difficult to provide relevant information. Check to be sure the interviewee has a clear understanding of your goals as well as your background. You might ask:

"Do you believe my objective and experience are clearly consistent? Are there areas which I should emphasize more strongly?"

When you are certain that the interviewee has understood your objective, proceed with your other questions. Make them brief but clear, and be sure that you give your interviewee time to respond. When you get your interviewees talking, you get them thinking and actively involved in your campaign.

Provide background on yourself, expertise, and relevant work history. Mention that before you actually commit to a new career field, you want to make sure it's compatible with your interests, skills, and goals. If you have already committed to this field or position, explain that you are making a job transition and want to present yourself in the best possible manner to potential employers. Ask for their professional opinions on what and how you've just presented yourself. Be prepared to take their suggestions graciously.

Your questions should be arranged in the following format, with two to five questions under each category:

1. Ice breaker, small talk to build rapport.
2. Questions about the individual as related to information you're seeking.
3. Questions about the industry: where it's going, current challenges.
4. Questions about your background summary; how the individual thinks your strengths and achievements can be utilized.
5. Networking/referral questions.

You should develop specific questions for each individual you see. Ask questions that are answerable by the interviewee; keep them within the same sphere of reference. It would be helpful to take a deductive approach, i.e., ask questions that generate a broader response and follow them with more specific ones to key in on ideas of particular interest. Remember, you will be conducting interviews with individuals who possess information critical to your successful marketing campaign. It is incumbent upon you to draw it to the surface. You should ask the following questions:

1. Do you think my objective is realistic, achievable, and clearly stated and supported?

2. Based on my background, which industries or types of companies or organizations would seem most appropriate for me to explore?

3. Are you aware of companies or industries that are in a growth or transitional position?

4. Are there any current trends or developments of which I should be aware?

5. What obstacles might I encounter? How can I overcome them?

6. Where would you see someone like myself fitting into a company such as yours? (Ask only where appropriate. For instance, you wouldn't ask this of a lawyer if you wanted to be in banking.) You can ask the interviewee's thoughts on these specific areas:

   ■ Responsibilities

   ■ Qualifications

   ■ Problems dealt with

   ■ Advancement

   ■ Training

   ■ Travel

   ■ Kinds of people who succeed/fail

   ■ Salary range/starting and long range potential

7. Are there any professional organizations I should join or publications I might want to read?

8. If you were me, how would you go about finding a new position?

9. Who are some people you would recommend I contact for information and advice?

Send Thank-You Letters and Follow-Up

Regardless of the outcome of the interview, always send a thank-you letter in which you genuinely express your gratitude for the individual's assistance. Reinforce any valuable information you were given and personalize the letter as much as possible. If the interviewee has given you names of referrals, be sure to follow-up by contacting these people by either telephone or letter. Assure your interviewee that you will soon follow-up on his or her referrals. An example of such a thank-you letter appears on page 68.

Is This Becoming a Job Interview?

Both informational and referral meetings should be under your control since you've set the agenda and managed the questions. You have initiated the contact, made the call, set the appointment, and have established yourself as the interviewer.

But nice things sometimes happen while talking with the decision makers. They may suddenly start to ask you leading questions, ask you about your background, and inquire about your skills. They talk about problems and wonder if you might be able to help. They start to talk about you as a member of the company, or they say that they could use someone like you. They take you to see other people in the company or give you a tour of the plant or offices.

These activities are sometimes called "Green Lights." They indicate that the decision makers are taking a great deal of interest in you that goes beyond just giving you information, advice, and referrals. They are beginning to see you as a resource; you suddenly become valuable to them.

What now? How do you handle this situation? Easily, but you must work at it. When you start getting "green lights," when they start asking you questions or begin telling you about their major problems and how they can't seem to solve them, take great notes and become very attentive to their probing and questioning. You have just crossed the wonderful barrier of not just being anybody, but becoming somebody who might be able to help them solve their problems.

Let the tone of the interview change to a quasi "job interview" without actively turning it into one yourself. Let them take control for awhile. Answer their questions, take the tour, show that you are defi-

Forty Questions to Ask in Referral Interviews

Most job hunters, realizing that networking is critical to their search, work hard to arrange face-to-face meetings with contacts. But setting up appointments with all the friends, professional acquaintances, and corporate bigwigs you can is just the first step. More important is knowing what to say once you arrive. Since wasting contacts' time is a no-no, you should prepare an agenda before each meeting. Decide what you'd like to find out from your contact, then prepare questions to elicit that information.

To simplify the query-writing process, review the following list of questions. Pick those that are most appropriate, then tailor them to fit your personal situation and speaking style. Formulate some of your own as well, but don't try to squeeze in too many questions. It's better to leave contacts wanting more than to wear out your welcome.

What Work is Like

1. Could you describe one of your typical workdays for me?

2. What skills are required in your position on a day-to-day basis?

3. What parts of your job do you find most challenging?

4. What do you find most enjoyable?

5. Are there any negatives to your job?

6. How many hours do you work in a typical week?

7. Which seasons of the year are toughest in your job?

8. How would you describe the corporate culture?

State of the Industry

9. Is this field growing enough that there's room for someone like me?

10. Are too many or too few people entering this profession?

11. What developments on the horizon could affect future opportunities?

12. This industry has changed dramatically in the past five years. What have you seen from inside your company? Where do you think the changes will happen in the next five years?

13. How frequently do layoffs occur? How does it affect the morale of employees?

14. Why do people leave this field or company?

15. Who are the most important people in the industry today?

16. Which companies have the best track record for promoting women and minorities?

17. Are there opportunities for self-employment in your field? Where?

Money and Advancement

18. What would be a reasonable salary range to expect if I entered this field? What is the long term potential?

19. What is the advancement potential in the field? What's a typical path?

20. How did you get your job?

21. If you could start all over again, would you change your career path in any way? Why?

22. How long does it take for managers to rise to the top?

23. What is the background of most senior-level executives?

Skills and Experience

24. What educational preparation would you recommend for someone who wants to advance in this field?

25. What qualifications do you seek in a new hire?

26. How do most people enter this profession?

27. Which of my skills are strong compared to other job hunters?

28. What do you think of the experience I've had so far? For what types of positions would it qualify me?

29. Can you recommend any courses I should take before proceeding?

30. What companies or industries do you think I should target?

Fitting In

31. Do you think my objective is clearly stated, realistic, and achievable?

32. Considering my background, how well do you think I would fit in this company and/or profession?

33. How does your company compare with others we've discussed?

34. Would the work involve any lifestyle changes, such as frequent travel or late-night business entertaining?

35. Considering all the people you've met in your line of work, what personal attributes are essential for success?

36. Taking into account my skills, education, and experience, what other career paths would you suggest I explore before making a decision?

More Information

37. Where can I write to get up-to-date information on salaries, employers, and industry issues?

38. What professional journals and organizations should I be aware of?

39. Is there anything else you think I need to know?

40. Who else would you recommend I speak with? When I call, may I use your name?

Sample Thank-You Letter
(Sent after an informational or referral meeting)

April 23, _____

Ms. Jessica Jones
Vice President, Client Executive
Frank Russell Investment Management Company
P.O. Box 1591
Tacoma, WA 98643

Dear Ms. Jones:

Thank you very much for taking time to see me yesterday. I thoroughly enjoyed our visit and discussion on the effects of a flat-tax on the stock market and especially on the mutual funds sector.

Your insights and information concerning the training and education required to become a "funds manager" in the financial world have really broadened my career scope and possibilities. The training looked intimidating at first, but your expert knowledge on how the profession operates has me more excited than ever about this possibility.

Your review of my background summary was very much appreciated. I will update the information and will forward a copy for your review and feedback within the next week.

I value your time and effort in assisting me in my career search and will keep you informed of my progress. You are a great ambassador for the "family" at Frank Russell.

* I will contact Mr. Robert Austin and Mr. David Chase as you suggested and I appreciate your referrals to these gentlemen.

Again, thank you for taking the time to talk with and advise me concerning my career opportunities.

Sincerely,

Roger Putnam
14893 East 46th Avenue
Spokane, WA 99212
(509) 922-4018
putnamr@aol.com

* To measure the quality of your progress in your campaign, you should be obtaining two referral names at the completion of each meeting. These names then lead to more, etc.

nitely interested in the company, but when the question about wanting to work there and how would you like to be considered for a position is given, maintain your integrity and return to the informational meeting mode. You did not come there asking for a job, so don't! But you may suggest another meeting to discuss the possibility of joining the firm. You may say something like this:

> "I'm flattered that you would even consider me as part of your company, but I really didn't come here today to ask you for a position and I won't compromise my integrity and do so. So we have two options. If you choose to stop this informational meeting and turn it into a job interview, you certainly have the authority to do so, or we could set another appointment to discuss this possibility later."

But the choice is yours! If this happens to you, remember not to ask for referrals. This will send a signal that you are not interested in working for them. After the meeting is over, set your date for your "job interview" and then do your homework to prepare for the interview. While the information is fresh, as soon as you leave, reflect and write down all pertinent information. Also, clarifying questions for the next interview date will show your attentiveness to detail. Make sure you are well prepared for the job interview.

6

PREPARE FOR THE
JOB INTERVIEW

Whether you are invited to a job interview because of the positive impression you made during one of your referral interviews or as result of sending your resume in response to an advertised position, you now have achieved what you have been working toward since you began your job search campaign—an interview! You will have the opportunity to determine whether this job opening is a good fit for your skills as well as demonstrate to the employer that your pattern of accomplishments makes you a good fit for the position and organization.

WHAT IS A JOB INTERVIEW?

When you are clearly being interviewed for a specific position, you are in a job interview. The interview may take any of the forms discussed in Chapter 4 or be a combination of more than one. Chances are you will go through more than one interview before you are offered the position. Except for entry-level positions, few offers are made during the first interview. Indeed, most of our clients go through multiple interviews—sometimes more than five—before receiving a job offer. So don't expect an offer at the first interview and don't be discouraged if after a second interview you still do not have a job offer. As long as there are future interviews scheduled or likely with the employer, you are still in the running. In fact, a greater number of interviews give both you and the employer more opportunities to determine whether the job is a good fit for your motivations and your skills. Keep an upbeat and positive manner throughout each interview—even your fourteenth interview with the very same company!

GOALS OF JOB INTERVIEWS

If we were to ask hundreds of job applicants what their goal is in the job interview, most would respond, with only slight variation in phrasing, that their goal is to sufficiently impress the interviewer so they are offered the job. At the same time, the goal of the interviewer is to identify the best person (the right person) who will be the solution to a specific organizational problem. The organization has a job to be done and needs someone to fill that need.

But interviews also have other goals. The most important goal for the job seeker should be to exchange information about him or herself, the position, and the organization. After all, you need good information in order to make a sound decision that will affect both your personal and professional lives. If you only focus on impressing the interviewer in order to get a job offer, you will most likely miss out on a great deal of critical information that will affect your future. You'll probably focus on providing answers to anticipated questions rather than asking questions that will elicit useful information about the position and organization so that you can make a decision as to whether or not this position is a good fit for both you and the employer. Individuals who primarily focus on impressing the interviewer with answers to questions are often surprised at what they discover during the first three months of the job—there is more to this so-called great job than what they learned during the interview. Many lament the fact that they didn't do enough research on the organization by asking important questions about the position and organization.

Most of our clients go through multiple interviews—sometimes more than five—before receiving a job offer.

There are only two ground rules for job interviews. You must:

1. Deal with the objectives and needs of both you and your interviewer; not one or the other, but both.
2. Retain control over the interview.

For many people, the job interview turns out to be a trap. The applicant's purpose is to get the job which meets his or her requirements, while the potential employer's purpose is to find a solution to his or her own problem. Both participants in the interview are centered on themselves and their own problems. They are separated by a desk and several miles of divergent interests. It is your job to close the gap during the interview.

Most job seekers turn control of a job interview over to the interviewer at the beginning of the meeting. This is unfair as well as unproductive. No interviewer can be fully aware of your purposes and goals, and no interviewer can produce useful results unless the goals of both participants are considered and met.

What should your purpose be at the first interview for a job? To get the job? Certainly not! To get a job offer? Equally unrealistic. Offers of jobs worth having are rarely made during the first interview. Despite this seemingly limited purpose of the first interview, its importance is crucial. It gives you an opportunity to find the interviewer's wavelength, to establish rapport on the human level. Your purpose is to establish rapport with the initial interviewer in order to be invited for the next interview. Acquire this mind-set:

1. I want to convey to the interviewer my skills and accomplishments as they relate to the needs of the employer.

2. I am here to determine if this is a place where I would like to work.

3. I have the right to meet the person who will be my boss.

GATHER DATA

Be sure you research the position, employer, and organization *before* you go to an interview. At the very minimum, you should know something about the position—the duties and responsibilities and salary range. You acquire this information by talking to fellow professionals and human resource personnel in other organizations as well as by examining data on such positions in salary studies available from professional associations and Web sites, such as those found on *http://jobsmart.org* and *www.abbott-langer.com*.

Never ever go into an interview and ask this killer question: "What do you do here?" Employers still report interviewees ask this stupid question which really indicates their level (or lack) of interest in the company! You should also research the company before going to an interview. Many useful resources on companies are readily available online and in libraries. For starters, examine *Moody's Industrial Manual, Moody's OTC, Moody's Municipal and Government Manual, Moody's Bank and Finance Manual, Moody's Public Utilities Manual, Moody's Transportation Manual,* and *Dun & Bradstreet.* Many companies publish newsletters and annual reports. Larger companies may have recruiting brochures or job hotlines. Larger libraries

> *Haldane clients have access to the proprietary Career Strategy 2000 electronic system which consists of a huge database of companies and opportunities.*

may have business database programs that contain indexes of thousands of magazines dating back ten years or more. Such programs contain press releases and news stories on local companies and may have an article on the company where you are interviewing—a great place to start your research. Haldane clients have access to the proprietary Career Strategy 2000 electronic system which consists of a huge database of companies and opportunities. Continue your search with annual reports, trade journals, Chamber of Commerce publications and newspapers. Utilize your network as a source on information. Contact members of your network and ask them about the company.

As you study the information you receive, prepare intelligent questions to ask during the job interview. Remember, your questions demonstrate your interest and "fit" in the organization and your eagerness to learn more about the responsibilities of the position and the future of the company. Indeed, the questions you ask based upon your knowledge of the company may impress the interviewer the most.

If you have difficulty acquiring information about the position and company prior to the interview, spend the first five minutes of the interview "doing research" by focusing on learning more about the company. Let the interviewer know you've attempted to get information on the company but you're unclear about certain things. Ask if they could briefly explain the position and business. By conducting research at this stage, you let the interviewer know that you are interested in the position and company and you may acquire some valuable information for both answering and asking questions.

FORMULATE EXAMPLES OF EFFECTIVENESS

Hopefully you've written a Haldane resume that clearly showcases your major strengths and accomplishments. Indeed, this resume may be the reason you were invited to the interview in the first place—you communicated a pattern of accomplishments desired by the prospective employer. Expect the interviewer to ask you questions about ability to do the job by probing your effectiveness in dealing with people, situations, and problems. Expect to be asked behavior-based questions that require you to give examples of your accomplishments as well as your decision-making style. Expect to deal with "What if" questions asking you to outline "What would you do if…" or "Give me an example of when you dealt with…" In anticipation of such questions, you should have a rich inventory of examples of your effectiveness based upon a list of accomplishments from which you wrote your resume. Be prepared to refer to these examples when asked about your effectiveness. Individuals with strong "story-telling" skills relating to examples of their effectiveness do very well in many of today's interview situations.

> *Expect to be asked behavior-based questions that require you to give examples of your accomplishments as well as your decision-making style.*

ANTICIPATE QUESTIONS AND STRATEGIZE RESPONSES

You should be prepared to answer certain questions based upon your knowledge of what questions interviewers are likely to ask. Many of the questions will relate to the contents of your resume, such as where and when you were employed, your educational background, employment time gaps, specific accomplishments, and major responsibilities. Others may deal with your personality and behavior. And still others may probe your decision-making capabilities, your weaknesses, and your attitude. Based on this and subsequent chapters, you should anticipate being asked certain questions.

Most important of all, you should practice responses to anticipated interview questions. In so doing, you should focus on developing a strategy for answering questions rather than memorizing specific answers. If you memorize, chances are you will be nervous and sound scripted. Your answers will not sound natural and the interviewer will detect a lack of spontaneity. Worse yet, you may forget! Your strategy should be to respond to each question in a positive manner that indicates your intelligence, tactfulness, enthusiasm, honesty, and interest in the position. Always avoid giving short "yes" and "no" responses to questions as well as lengthy responses that may lose the listener's interest and attention. Try to use **positive language** that emphasizes your capabilities rather than negative language that may raise questions about your judgment. For example, if you were fired from your last job and the interviewer asks you why you left, avoid going into any nasty details about the affair. Instead of speaking ill about your previous company, employer, or co-workers, use a strategy that emphasizes that you made an error and have learned from it:

> "The job was not a good fit for either me or the employer. I made a mistake in accepting the position by not asking the right questions about the company's financial position and the people I would be working with. In the end, we decided it would be in both of our interests to part company. I learned an important lesson: Ask the right questions before accepting a position. I won't make that mistake again."

If asked why you completed three years of undergraduate studies but didn't graduate, develop a positive response. Rather than say you didn't like college or you flunked out because of your extreme social life, be positive and focus on the present;

> "While I learned a great deal from my college years, I decided what I really wanted to do in finance did not require a college degree. I needed a mentor and experience. I was lucky to be offered a position with C. L. Polsby at the end of my junior year. The timing was right. During the past ten years I've moved into several key financial positions based upon my performance. I'm glad to say that I've never felt my lack of a college degree has affected my career."

If you are asked about your weaknesses, avoid confessing any perceived weaknesses on your part not denying that you have any weaknesses. Your strategy should be to focus on the positive, such as turning a potential weakness into a strength, rather than confess your negatives. For example, if asked "We all have weaknesses. What are some of yours?" some interviewees might honestly respond in this manner:

> *If you develop a strategy that focuses on emphasizing your positive qualities in relationship to the job in question, you should be able to answer most questions well. Try to eliminate any negative language, such as "didn't," "can't," or "won't."*

"I have a tendency to say 'yes' to too many things and thus take on too many projects at the same time. I'm learning to better prioritize my work and say "no" when appropriate. As a result, I'm better able to get projects completed on time and focus on what's really important to my work."

Again, the important point here is not to memorize answers to anticipated interview questions. If you develop a strategy that focuses on emphasizing your positive qualities in relationship to the job in question, you should be able to answer most questions well. Try to eliminate any negative language, such as "didn't," "can't,' or "won't."

FRAME QUESTIONS TO ASK

Many employers report the best candidates are ones that ask thoughtful questions. Indeed, many employers focus on the quality of a candidate's questions rather than on the content of his answers. Asking questions during the interview enables you to (1) conduct additional research on the company and (2) express your interest in the company and position. Individuals who fail to ask questions often appear to lack interest and enthusiasm. They are more oriented to getting the job offer than to exchanging information about themselves and the position. When asked "Do you have any questions?" be sure to be prepared with several questions about the company and position that indicate your interest and enthusiasm. Avoid any questions about the salary and benefits since such questions may give the interviewer the wrong impression—you're primarily interested in compensation. Focus, instead, on clarifying expectations about the position—whom you would be working with, extent of your responsibilities, where the company sees you in five years, and company goals and challenges. All questions concerning compensation should be left to the very end—after you have been offered the job.

REHEARSE

Prior to the interview, you should rehearse possible interview scenarios, form answering questions to asking questions. Put together a list of anticipated interview questions, and practice how you would respond to each. Make sure you include some tough "What if" and behavior-based questions that require you to relate stories about your performance as well as any questions relating to perceived weaknesses on your part—time gaps, job-hopping, limited advancement, unemployment. Again, you should not try to memorize answers to each question. You want to focus on a **strategy** that results in positive, enthusiastic, spontaneous, and memorable responses. You may want to role-play with a friend who serves as the interviewer. Tape record your conversation. Listen to how you answer each question. Do you sound spontaneous, positive, enthusiastic, and likable? Are your answers complete, interesting, and commanding attention? Overall, do you sound like someone you would want to hire?

Be sure you also put together a list of thoughtful questions to ask the interviewer. These questions should be geared toward eliciting important information about the company and position as well as communicating your continuing interest in the job. Remember, the quality of the questions you ask may leave the most lasting positive impression on the interviewer. Take this list of questions with you to the interview. When asked "Do you have any questions" it's perfectly acceptable to take out your list of questions and refer to them by first asking "Yes, I do. In fact, I've written down a few questions to make sure I don't forget them. If you don't mind, let me refer to my notes." This action also indicates you have come well prepared for the interview.

PLAN YOUR IMAGE

Image counts more than you may think. According to a 1994 survey conducted by *Executive Recruiters,* corporate executives **reject** more than 80 percent of job applicants strictly based on their inappropriate attire. The first thing about an applicant to make an impression on the interviewer is the candidate's physical appearance and dress. How you look—your clothing and accessories, your hairstyle, facial hair (if any), make-up (women), your physical bearing, your facial expression—conveys messages, either positive or negative. During the first few seconds of any initial encounter, before you ever open your mouth to speak, you will make a lasting impression on the interviewer by how you dress and handle yourself nonverbally. Therefore, it is very important you plan to make your initial impression on the interviewer a positive one. On the list of "28 Job Interview Knockouts" appearing at the end of this chapter, poor personal appearance ranks number 1! Who can believe "dressing for success" isn't important?

Matching or exceeding the expectations of the interviewer regarding your physical appearance and dress is not meant to compensate for a lack of qualifications. Rather, assuming you already have the qualifications (or you would not have been invited to the interview), your appropriate choice of wardrobe and grooming will give you the extra edge over other applicants who may be more careless.

MAKE THE FIRST FIVE MINUTES COUNT FOR YOU

Many of the hiring officials we talk with indicate they are usually able to determine within the first five minutes—often in much less time—whether they want to invite the applicant back for a second interview. What can employers respond to in such a short time? Certainly they have not had the opportunity to determine much of anything about the interviewee's qualifications that were not already apparent on the resume. Whether consciously or not, employers are looking for individuals that fit their corporate image. Will you fit into their organization? Will you work well with your superiors and subordinates? Will you represent the organization well to their clients or the public?

Your goal is to fit the expectations employers have for the individuals they hire to work within their organization and to represent the organization to others. If your appearance doesn't fit the interviewer's expectations, at the very least it will be a distraction throughout the interview—which means the interviewer will not be giving full attention to the many strengths you try to convey. Even worse, the interviewer is likely to conclude that you don't belong in their organization. You are not like them. You will not fit in nor be a good representative for the organization. Whether you want to believe it or not, employers actually make judgments about your competence and value based on how you look! People who are appropriately dressed and well groomed are found to be better liked and thought to be more intelligent and competent!

PREPARE FOR SEVERAL INTERVIEWS

Haldane Associates suggestions on attire do not assume that all executives dress well. In fact, many do not by our standards. However, the higher people go up the corporate ladder, the more important their personal attire becomes. By not dressing well you may offend interviewers. You convey the message that either you do not know how to dress appropriately and thus will not represent the company well, or that this interview was not important enough for you to dress to your potential.

> *The higher people go up the corporate ladder, the more important their personal attire becomes. By not dressing well you may offend interviewers.*

Before launching your job campaign, assess your entire wardrobe. You should have several appropriate interview outfits because you can expect to go through a series of two, three or more interviews with each organization where you are a serious candidate. Avoid wearing what appears to be the same outfit twice in succession with the same organization.

If you are starting out with few items in your wardrobe that are right for a job interview and money is a concern, buy the very best suit you can afford and accessorize it in a variety of ways to make it appear to be different attire. Buy two suits if you can, but one good quality suit, carefully chosen, will serve you better than two cheap looking suits. This advice, to buy fewer good quality items rather than several cheap appearing articles of clothing, applies to both men and women. If you shop for sales in quality stores, you may be able to make your budget stretch further.

If you can only buy one good quality suit, what should it look like? If you are male, select a classic styled, dark navy blue (solid color—no pinstripes on this one), single breasted suit. The fabric should be wool or a wool blend. The buttons should match the suit color—no metal buttons. Metal buttons on the jacket will be a give-away that you are wearing the same suit over again. There should be no detailing anywhere on the suit that calls attention to itself. In other words, it should blend in rather than stand out. Even the good quality will blend in with the quality likely being worn by the executives who interview you and the quality they are used to seeing worn by their associates.

Wear your suit with a white long-sleeved shirt and use a variety of good quality neckties (see next section for more on shirts and neckties) to give you the look of different outfits. If you have carefully selected your suit, you could wear it with the same white shirt for every interview—assuming the shirt is a basic plain cotton broadcloth with barrel cuffs (buttoned) and it has been freshly laundered for each wearing. Vary your neckties and only you will likely know how much of your outfit is the same!

The advice for women is similar. Buy the best you can afford and buy fewer good quality outfits rather than several marginal ones. You can choose an option similar to the one outlined above for men. If you are buying just one good suit, select a dark neutral colored suit—solid navy is the best choice because other colors are more likely to call attention to themselves. Navy suits on both men and women are so common in the boardroom that your suit is unlikely to be noticed if you pay attention to the details of styling. The best fabric choice is wool or a wool blend. The jacket and skirt should be conservative and classic in cut with no detailing that calls attention to itself: no epaulets, no trim or top stitching of another color, no form fitting or short cut jacket or skirt. The buttons should be the same color as the suit. Avoid a double-breasted jacket; it will be more likely to call attention to the fact that you are wearing the same suit more than once.

> *Buy the best you can afford and buy fewer good quality outfits rather than several marginal ones.*

Wear your navy suit with a variety of different colored silk blouses—red, blue, maroon, cream or white—would provide enough difference that only you are likely to realize that your suit is the same. If you also accessorize your blouses a bit differently—perhaps a beautiful silk scarf in the neckline of a blouse for one interview and a gold "panther" link necklace in the open neckline of your blouse for another interview—you further disguise the fact that you are wearing one suit for more than one interview.

For both men and women, the above advice is to select suits that will not stand out by calling attention to themselves. Similar advice would be given even if you were buying several suits to wear for your interviews. However, attention to the detailing on your interview suit is especially critical for you to successfully conceal the fact you are wearing the same suit to several interviews!

SELECT ATTIRE TO CONVEY COMPETENCE: MEN

A good rule of thumb is that you want your attire to fit in—not stand out. Except for a position in a theatrical production or similar venue, if you wear something so flamboyant that after you have left the interview it is all anyone talks about, you have most probably lost the opportunity for the job. Your appearance should be in sync with the organization and its executives' expectations. Dress to your potential. If you are applying for a corporate position, you must look the part. The higher up the corporate ladder you are climbing, the more important this becomes. For the most part, it is difficult to overdress for the job interview.

Basics

A dark gray or navy suit will convey the most professional and authoritative look. These colors provide the power dressing for your interviews and for those occasions once you land the job when you need an extra edge to further your look of credibility.

A white shirt is your most professional attire, although if you purposely choose to lower your power image a bit, a medium to light blue shirt has long been a mainstay of corporate America. Although other colored shirts enjoy popularity and are in fashion from time to time, save them for once you land the job. If after you get the job, you look at what others are wearing and decide other colored shirts are appropriate for your organization, that is your choice. But consider carefully the messages you wish to convey. Just because others are wearing the latest fashion statement doesn't mean that choice projects the best image for your climb up the corporate ladder. Buy quality silk ties. Select a tie that coordinates with your shirt and suit and looks corporate. No large artsy prints or large floral patterns that are reminiscent of Hawaiian shirts—even if they are all over the store when you shop. A classic stripe or rep (small repeat design) tie is a good choice to project stability and a conservative image. Avoid bow ties—they stand out rather than fit in.

If you have had your suits and neckties for a very long time, make sure the width of the lapels on the jacket and the width of the tie are current. Although men's conservative business attire changes ever so slightly, change does take place over time. If your attire is dated, it will probably be apparent to the interviewer.

Make certain everything fits and is in good repair—no missing buttons or jacket hem held in place with a safety pin. Everything you put on for the interview should be freshly cleaned or pressed. Your shirt should be fresh from the laundry and be pressed—even if the label states *wash and wear*. A pressed shirt looks neat and crisp and conveys to the wearer a more enhanced image than a rumpled shirt. Your suit may only need to be pressed, but have it cleaned if it shows any sign of dirt or stains.

> *Dark shoes are a must, with black laced shoes—wingtips or not—being the first choice of corporate boardrooms.*

Your dress leather shoes should be clean and shined and have soles that do not show excessive wear. If there are signs of excessive wear, buy a new pair or visit your local shoe repair shop. Dark shoes are a must, with black laced shoes—wingtips or not—being the first choice of corporate boardrooms. Socks should be a dark color—ideally matching the color of the shoe. Socks should be calf length—high enough so that there is no leg showing if you cross your legs during the interview.

Accessories

Accessories are also on display and convey messages about the wearer. Leave your sports watch with its large dial, and colorful band at home. Your dress watch should be thin and elegant. A yellow gold watch-band or a dark leather strap are good choices. White gold or silver watch-bands tend to be big and bulky and be attached to sports type watches; however, if yours is attached to an elegant dress watch and adds to your positive image it is an acceptable choice. Your look will be better enhanced if you keep your metal colors the same. If you wear yellow gold rings, your look is more enhanced with a gold than with a silver colored watch. If your rings and watch are yellow gold, select a leather belt with a gold colored buckle or you can wear a belt with a leather covered buckle. Carry a yellow gold colored pen to complete the monochromatic metal ensemble. Leave plastic pens or pens with logos from the hotels where you have stayed at home!

Your eyeglasses and frames should be clean, in good repair, and if they have metal frames, your best look will be achieved by following the rule to keep all the metal colors you wear the same. Avoid dark lenses or exaggerated frames. Dark lenses hide you from the interviewer. How can your eyes convey enthusiasm if the interviewer cannot see them? Exaggerated frames will distract the interviewer from your message and will make you stand out rather than fit in!

Be very careful when using colognes and shaving lotions. If you use them, select a light scent and apply sparingly. Similar to perfumes for women, heavy colognes and shaving lotions for men can be very offensive and thus a real killer in the interview.

A leather case to carry an extra copy of your resume, your list of references, the questions you have formulated to ask during the interview, and any other paperwork you wish to have with you at the interview, adds to the look of professionalism. A white notepad to take notes during the interview looks better than a yellow legal pad. Tuck the white pad of paper inside the leather case as well.

If the weather makes an overcoat or umbrella necessary, make sure these convey positive statements about you as well. A dark wool or wool blend overcoat for cold weather or a tan lightweight coat for less cold weather along with a full sized black umbrella will serve you well.

Avoid collapsible umbrellas. They simply don't add to your image and credibility the way a full sized umbrella does.

Even though you want your overcoat and umbrella to convey positive images to those who see you wearing them, do not wear them into the actual interview itself. Leave them in a coat room or the outer office if possible. If there is no place to leave them, then take the coat off and carry it in with you. Put it on an empty chair. Do not wear your overcoat during the interview. You will not look as if you belong. You will appear to be there temporarily, which is not the message you want to convey.

SELECT ATTIRE TO CONVEY COMPETENCE: WOMEN

Important as choice of attire is for men, choice of attire is even more important for a woman going to a job interview. Like it or not, the reality is that some interviewers still view a woman as less competent than a male—simply because of her gender! Since physical appearance and dress are the first thing the interviewer notices, getting the extra edge the right attire and grooming provide can make the candidate a more likely winner right from the start.

Basics

No matter what anyone may tell you, your most powerful and professional attire is a skirted suit. Yes, a tailored dress is acceptable business attire—the operative word is acceptable. A dress will not do nearly as much to enhance your professional image as will a business suit. Navy will provide one of the best looks for those situations when you really need an authoritative look, and everyone can wear navy. If you have soft coloring select a shade of navy that does not appear nearly black. You can soften the effect of the dark color with the color of the blouse you pair with it. If you have soft coloring, avoid the stark contrast of navy with a pure white blouse. If you want contrast, select a beige instead. Or go with less contrast and wear a maroon or medium blue blouse. Soft gray or maroon colored suits can work well, but are a bit less powerful. The best fabric for your suit is wool or a wool-blend with the look and feel of wool. The suit should not look so fashion forward that it calls attention to itself or will be out-dated in six months. Timeless, classic styling is your best choice. A skirt length that is at the knee (slightly above or below—depending on the length that is good on you) adds to your professional look.

A long-sleeved silk blouse or a fabric that looks like silk will pair well with your business suit. At present, blouses left open at the neck with collars tailored like those on men's shirts are prevalent. Worn either with a scarf tucked in the open collar or a tailored gold necklace similar to the "panther" styling, these blouses look both professional and stylish.

Stockings that are skin tone are best with most outfits. Avoid stockings that are darker than your skintone—an exaggerated suntan on only your legs looks strange—or too reddish in tone for your skin. If you are wearing a navy skirted suit and navy shoes, sheer navy stockings can pull the two together and

No matter what anyone may tell you, your most powerful and professional attire is a skirted suit. Navy will provide one of the best looks for those situations when you really need an authoritative look, and everyone can wear navy.

give your professional outfit a polished look. Other than navy, do not wear any other color of hosiery other than a natural skin tone, and then wear navy only if both your skirt and shoes are navy!

Your shoes should not be lighter than the hem of your skirt. Lighter colored shoes will direct the interviewer's eyes to your feet and that is not where the attention should be focused! A shoe color that matches the skirt color is always good: a navy skirt paired with navy shoes or a brown skirt paired with brown shoes. Your best basic (will go with anything color) shoe color is one that visually picks up your hair or skin color. If you have brown hair and are wearing a suit in a color that you have no shoes to match, wear brown shoes. Visually the color on your feet will relate to a color you are wearing—your hair. If you have blond hair, a light camel or beige colored shoe can visually repeat your hair or skin color. Black is a good basic color choice for a woman who has black hair. A basic tailored pump, with a medium heel height, is the best shoe style to complement your business suit. Make certain your leather shoes are polished, or brushed if you wear sueded leather. Avoid flats, platform-soled shoes, clogs, boots or sandals for interviews.

Make certain all your clothing fits and is in good repair. If a hem or a button needs to be sewn, do it before the day of the interview. Everything you put on for the interview should be freshly cleaned or pressed. No make-up on the blouse collar nor dirt on the sleeve cuffs. Have your suit cleaned or pressed—depending on need.

Accessories

Accessories should be classic and limited in number. In general jewelry that dangles—whether earrings or a bracelet—is better reserved for other settings. Keep your metal colors the same. If you wear a yellow gold ring, then select your earrings, watch or any pin or necklace you may wear in yellow gold. Any buttons or a belt that has metal showing should also be yellow gold. Diamonds may be a girl's best friend, but except for a diamond engagement ring or wedding band, avoid wearing glittering jewelry to a job interview.

If you wear eyeglasses with metal frames, your best look will be achieved by following the rule to keep your metal colors the same. Your eyeglasses and frames should be clean and in good repair. Avoid dark lenses or exaggerated frames. Dark lenses hide you from the interviewer. How can you convey enthusiasm if the interviewer cannot see your eyes? Exaggerated frames will distract the interviewer from your message and will make you stand out rather than fit in!

For the interview, make-up should be discreet. You do need to wear some make-up. It helps balance the visual weight of the business suit and if properly applied will give you a finished and polished look. A make-up base that exactly matches your skin tone at the point where your face meets your neck, eye-liner lightly applied, mascara, a bit of blush and lipstick and you should be set to go! The mascara should be lightly applied and the color should be no darker than your natural hair/lash color. Do not use black mascara if your hair is brown. It will be too harsh on you and you will cheapen your look. You are getting ready for a job interview—but not for the oldest profession! Your fingernails should be impeccably clean and are best polished with a clear polish.

> *If you do wear fragrance, select a light scent, and spray it sparingly. Heavy perfumes can be very offensive and thus a real killer in the interview.*

We recommend that you not use perfume. If you do wear fragrance, select a light scent, and spray it sparingly. Heavy perfumes can be very offensive and thus a real killer in the interview.

You will probably carry either a handbag or a briefcase to your interview. Ideally, either one should be leather and in a color that repeats a color you are wearing so that it relates to your overall visual image. The color could be navy if you are wearing a navy suit to the interview or it could visually pick-up your hair color. A brown briefcase/handbag is a good choice for a woman who has brown hair. She can carry it with any outfit and it will go with what she is wearing—her hair! Decide to carry one or the other—briefcase or handbag—rather than both. You can place items you would normally carry in your handbag in the briefcase or carry a small clutch purse tucked inside your briefcase. This leaves one hand free for that important handshake!

You may also wish to carry a small leather case inside your briefcase with an extra copy of your resume tucked inside along with your list of references, the questions you have formulated to ask during the interview, and any other paperwork you may need. Take a white notepad on which to take notes. A white pad looks better than a yellow one. If the pad is in a leather case, it will look even better.

If you wear a coat to the interview, take it off once you arrive. Leave your coat or umbrella in the outer office if possible. If there is no place to leave them, carry them with you, but put them on a chair once you are in the interview room. You want to separate yourself from the coat and umbrella. They both say you are there temporarily, which is not the message you want to convey.

LOOK YOUR BEST AT ALL TIMES

You never know when you will meet someone who could be important to your career advancement—you meet someone on the golf course or when you are picking your child up from day care. It turns out this person heads the department where you have an interview scheduled the following day!

Male or female, have your hair cut regularly. Most men find that a cut every three weeks will keep their hair looking great. Women may need to have a trim every four weeks. Make sure your hair is impeccably clean and styled to look good on you as well as be appropriate for a business setting. Your teeth should be white. If years of stains from

28 Job Interview Knockouts

There are many things you can say and do that can knock you out of consideration for a job offer. Do any of the following and you may be politely shown the door with this unenthusiastic closing: "Thanks for coming. We'll call you if we have any further questions."

1. Presents a poor personal appearance, from dress to grooming

2. Projects an overbearing, over-aggressive, "know-it-all" posture

3. Expresses incomplete thoughts

4. Speaks poorly—problems with voice, diction, grammar

5. Lacks career planning—no objective apparent

6. Acts passive or indifferent—no clear purpose or goal

7. Lacks confident attitude—too nervous and ill-at-ease

8. Makes excuses, appears evasive, and hedges when asked sensitive questions about background

9. Speaks ill of previously employers

10. Maintains poor eye contact

11. Offers a limp, fishy handshake

12. Expresses no interest in company nor having done research on the company or industry

13. Arrives late for the interview

14. Asks about salary and benefits too soon and too often

15. Lacks courtesy and is ill-mannered

16. Projects a cynical attitude

17. Tries to be humorous with inappropriate jokes and irritating laughter

18. Drops names and emphasizes "who I know"

19. Expresses intolerance and strong prejudices

20. Smokes or chews gum

21. Complains

22. Fails to express appreciation for the interviewer's time

23. Talks about personal problems and financial needs

24. Ends with an inappropriate and presumptuous closing, such as "When can I start?"

25. Wears heavy perfume, cologne, or shaving lotion

26. Appears very self-centered by asking questions relevant to his or her needs rather than to the employer's needs

27. Offers very short answers to questions—appears to lack substance, interest, and enthusiasm

28. Does not ask questions about the job or employer

food or smoking have stained your teeth, consider having them professionally bleached by your dentist. There are toothpastes on the market which claim to whiten teeth, but if these don't work well enough for you, talk to your dentist. It should not have to be said, but shower every day and use an antiperspirant.

Our recommendations emphasize that you achieve a total look which is well groomed and understated as opposed to being overly faddish or contemporary. Our years of experience with our clients reinforces that employers are comfortable with and trust those individuals whom they perceive to be like them. Executives believe—perhaps subconsciously— that individuals who meet their expectations are more credible both in terms of their expertise and trustworthiness. If you dress to meet the interviewer's expectations, you will feel more comfortable knowing that you look perfect for the interview situation. The interviewer will feel comfortable with your appearance which makes him/her feel you are like them; you are one of them; you will fit into the organization. Your image will complement your job skills and the employer will be able to give full attention to the strengths you are trying to convey.

PROJECT AN IMAGE OF CONFIDENCE AND COMPETENCE

The initial impression you make on the interviewer is created by your physical appearance and dress. A lasting impression is also created by your body language. Your bearing must convey confidence. Whether you enter an office to indicate your arrival to the receptionist or to meet the interviewer, maintain an erect posture with your head (chin) up and your shoulders back. Walk with a purposeful, confident stride.

Initiate the handshake when meeting the interviewer—it will add to your appearance of self-confidence and competence as well. Extend your hand, grasp the interviewer's hand firmly web to web, shake once or twice and release.

Maintain eye contact with the interviewer about 80 percent of the time—particularly when the other person is speaking. When you are thinking about a response or responding, you may find your eye contact with the interviewer is a bit less. But you need to "connect" with the interviewer and a major part of the connection is established through eye contact. Our language is rife with sayings that indicate the importance of eye contact from our saying that someone has "shifty eyes" to indicating that an individual couldn't "look us in the eye." Lack of eye contact is a negative!

> *Maintain eye contact with the interviewer about 80 percent of the time—particularly when the other person is speaking.*

Remember interviewers are people too. They tend to hire people whom they like and whom they feel they can trust. They want to hire someone who is enthusiastic about the job and the company. Convey your self-confidence, enthusiasm and likability and if you also have the technical qualifications, the job offer is likely yours!

PLOT YOUR ROUTE

It may seem obvious, but arriving on time is really important! One of the first impressions you don't want to make is to arrive late for the interview. However, it's surprising how many interviewees do arrive late, make lame or inappropriate excuses ("Your directions were not very clear"), and expect the interviewer to forgive them for what appears to be such a minor transgression. Some call the interviewer at the time of the interview-or ten minutes after it was to begin—to admit they are lost and ask for directions.

If you arrive late for an interview, accept the fact that you'll never be able to overcome this negative first impression. You appear irresponsible and disorganized. The interviewer is left to wonder: "If this is the candidate's best effort to arrive at an important meeting, how will he or she do on the job? Late to work? Late for appointments? Lots of excuses for not panning ahead of time?"

Therefore, it's important that you know exactly where you need to be for the interview. Where exactly will the interview take place? What route should you take, and how many traffic lights should you anticipate? What type of parking situation are you likely to encounter? How long will it take to find parking and then go from the parking area to the office? The best way to answer these questions is to literally drive to the interview site the day before the interview at about the same time of day to test how long it will take to get to the

> *Plan to arrive at least 15–20 minutes early so you will have time to compose yourself and perhaps engage the receptionist in small talk and read some of the company literature available in the reception area.*

location. Plot your route so that you arrive in plenty of time. Plan to arrive at least 15-20 minutes early so you will have time to compose yourself and perhaps engage the receptionist in small talk and read some of the company literature available in the reception area. Visit the restroom to check your attire and hair in the mirror. Arrive early so you can make a positive first impression.

THE DAY OF THE
JOB INTERVIEW

Some things that could be done on the day of the job interview can create less stress if taken care of prior to the day of the interview. By attending to these things early, you assure that they are done properly rather than haphazardly in a last minute rush. By being prepared ahead of time, you can better maintain your cool head and your confident manner. If you do not do the following things prior to the day of your interview, by all means set your alarm early enough to give yourself time to adequately take care of them. The Boy Scout motto, "Be Prepared," definitely applies!

BE PREPARED

It helps to have some of the little things done so you don't have to worry about them the day of the interview. Certainly you should know how to get to the place where the interview will take place. Make sure you have plenty of gasoline in your car as well as money for parking and lunch. Probably better to choose the parking garage over the parking meter on the street. Neither worrying about whether you are about to get a ticket nor leaving the interview to put more money in the meter will enhance your image. Lunch money could become important if the interviewer suggests that you continue the interview over lunch—perhaps along with other office staff. If lunch is in the company cafeteria, your credit card probably won't do much good. It would be embarrassing to have to ask the interviewer to borrow lunch money!

If possible, select your clothing several days prior to your interview. This will give you time to take clothing to be pressed or cleaned if necessary, polish your shoes, as well as sew that missing button back on your suit jacket! Pull together copies of your background summary, your resume, a list of references, as well as any job history data which you might need if you are asked to complete a job application. Make sure you have a pen and a notepad.

Memorize the name of the person who will be interviewing you until you know it nearly as well as your own. It is embarrassing to forget or mispronounce the name of the interviewer. If you forget or mispronounce the interviewer's name, no matter how well you handle this slip, it makes a negative first impression and first impressions are lasting!

ARRIVE EARLY: FIRST IMPRESSIONS COUNT

You never have a second chance to make a first impression. So make sure the first impression the interviewer has of you is a positive one! In many ways the first five minutes are the most important of the interview. When you first meet, the interviewer makes initial decisions as to whether he/she likes you, whether you will fit into the organization, and whether you will be able to deal effectively with their clients. Detailed information about your background will come out later, but this information will be weighed against the first impressions that have already been formed.

> *You never have a second chance to make a first impression. In many ways the first five minutes are the most important of the interview.*

The easiest way to make a negative initial impression is to arrive late for the interview! If you miss those important first five minutes, it will be very difficult to turn that negative impression into a positive one during the remainder of the interview.

Make sure you know where you are going for the interview and the route to get there. Leave yourself plenty of time—allowing for possible unexpected delays due to road repairs that create detours or accidents that slow traffic to a standstill. Allow time to find parking and to clear corporate security. Many companies as well as government offices have instituted security procedures that take time to sign in and go through.

Leave yourself enough time so that you can find the building, locate parking, sign in and clear security and be at the office where you are to meet the interviewer 15-20 minutes before your scheduled appointment time. That will leave you at least 5 minutes to visit the rest room and do a last minute check of your appearance before actually arriving at the receptionist's desk. If your trip has gone smoothly with no unexpected delays, you may find yourself at the interview site extremely early. This is far better than arriving late, but you do not want to arrive so early that you make people feel uncomfortable—this is most likely to happen in small companies—or leave them wondering if you have nothing else to do with yourself. If you arrive really early, park your car and sit in it, using the time to review notes you have on the company or reviewing your strategies for the interview. You don't want to drive around 'to kill time" at this point as you might encounter delays that will make you late for the interview.

Introduce Yourself With a Smile

Make certain the receptionist or administrative assistant knows you are there. Greet this person with an appropriate "Good morning" or "Good afternoon" followed by your name and the time of your appointment. "Good morning. I'm John Hanley. I have a ten o'clock appointment with Mr. Jones." Do not be so presumptuous as to call the interviewer by his or her first name. Even if you have known this individual for years, at this point keep your association on a professional level and use the person's surname.

Your Behavior Speaks Volumes

The receptionist will probably ask you to be seated in the reception area while you await your meeting with the interviewer. As you wait, use the time to your advantage. Are there materials about the corporation available? Pick them up and read about the company. This serves two purposes. First, you appear to be interested in the company which conveys positive messages about your sense of purpose. Second, you may pick up significant information about the firm which will help you form better responses as well as ask better questions during the interview.

If the company newsletter appears to be introducing a lot of new managers to employees, you might raise a question during the interview about the company's retention of key people. Besides providing useful background for your questioning of the interviewer, upon later reflection you may decide that this organization seems to be having a lot of problems with personnel and that it is not a good fit for you!

Good preparation for the job interview should have told you much about the company already. But insightful reading of corporate brochures and newsletters may uncover information that you have not yet come across in your research of the firm.

YOUR BEARING SHOULD EXUDE CONFIDENCE

As you meet and greet the interviewer, your bearing should exude confidence, not arrogance, but self-confidence. If the interviewer comes out to greet you and takes you back to his office, stand up to full height, smile, and extend your hand as you use his name and indicate how glad you are to have the opportunity to meet with him. Grasp his hand firmly, shake once or twice, and then let go. Follow him to his office or the conference room where the interview will take place and remain standing until he indicates where you should be seated. In general, wait until asked to be seated before you sit. However, if for any reason, he seems not to be going to do this and so much time has elapsed as to be uncomfortable, take a seat that looks the most appropriate. You might even ask, "Is this where you would like me to sit?"

The receptionist may announce that, "Mr. Jones will see you now. Please follow me." In this instance follow the receptionist with a purposeful gait, shoulders back and head straight. When you meet Mr. Jones, smile, extend your hand, grasp his hand firmly, shake once or twice and release. Use his name as you indicate that you are pleased to meet with him. Wait for him to indicate where you should be seated.

SMALL TALK COUNTS

During the first few minutes of the interview the participants usually engage in small talk. Topics range from whether the applicant had any trouble finding the interview location to the weather or may involve discussion of mutual acquaintances or outside areas of interest. A photo of the interviewer proudly showing off the big fish he caught could start a conversation on a mutual interest if the interviewee was also an avid fisherman.

Whatever you are asked about your drive to the site of the interview, indicate that you had no trouble finding the place at all. You can comment about the dastardly weather if you wish but that is about as negative as you should get—after all neither you nor the employer has control over the weather. But it is difficult to talk about the horrible time you had finding the place of the interview without making yourself or the employee who gave you directions sound less intelligent than either might wish. There is no need to badmouth one of the company's employees and it may have been the interviewer who put the directions together, nor should you volunteer that you were unable to follow directions!

Whatever course the small talk takes, do not dismiss it as insignificant. The interviewer is already forming impressions of you and how well you will fit into this organization. The more common ground you establish, the better the rapport, and the better the fit will seem to the interviewer. The compatibility between you and the interviewer is the important foundation upon which you will build as you establish your competence throughout the remaining stages of the interview.

RESPONDING TO THE INTERVIEWER'S QUESTIONS

Listen carefully to the questions posed by the interviewer. If you are unsure of the intention or if the question, as phrased, seems too broad, ask for clarification. For example, if the interviewer begins by asking you to, "Tell me about yourself." You may wish to narrow the focus, by asking a question in return. If you are applying for a position in which management ability is a primary prerequisite, you might respond with, "Would you prefer that I discuss the various management positions I have held or focus on my management style?" This tactic gives you a chance to think as well as get a sense of what the questioner is looking for. He may either specify one of the choices you suggested or may suggest a different line of interest. Either way, you can narrow your response to an area of the interviewer's interest.

> *Whatever course the small talk takes, do not dismiss it as insignificant. The more common ground you establish, the better the rapport, and the better the fit will seem to the interviewer.*

Although this is easier said than done, try to forget yourself and "how you are doing." Focus on the interviewer and his or her needs.

Respond to questions with supporting data—give evidence of what you have accomplished or how you have handled a type of problem. Supporting data makes your answer more credible, more interesting, and more memorable to the interviewer than just a response that you have done something. Go to your interview prepared with examples of your accomplishments. Tell stories but remember to keep them short and to the point. Responses that exceed two minutes will soon lose the attention of the listener unless there is something in your response that is particularly riveting. Give examples of how you turned around the production department in your present (or most recent) position. Cite figures that support your statement that you increased sales or decreased customer complaints. Be specific when it is possible and is in your best interest. Be prepared to tell when, how, and where you used a particular skill to achieve specific goals or produce specific results for a previous employer.

> *Go to your interview prepared with examples of your accomplishments. Tell stories but remember to keep them short and to the point. Responses that exceed two minutes will soon lose the attention of the listener.*

Whatever your past accomplishments, try to tie them to what you can do in the future for the company where you are interviewing. Be explicit in making the connection to the job under consideration if you can. You can demonstrate your understanding of the job and avoid leaving it to chance that the interviewer will make the connection.

See Chapter 8 for specific examples and strategies for dealing with answers to tough interview questions. Remember that you do your hardest work before you arrive at the interview. If you have thoroughly researched the organization and, if possible, the person who will be conducting the interview; anticipated questions you are likely to be asked; and determined the strategies you will use as you respond, you have laid the groundwork for an effective interview. Remember to explicitly draw the connection between your past accomplishments and the competencies you would bring to your new organization.

YOU SHOULD ASK QUESTIONS TOO

But your work is not over until, as part of the preparation for the interview, you formulate questions you want to ask of the interviewer. These questions are designed to elicit information that will help you later as you determine whether you are interested in working for the organization. If you are later offered the position, this information will also help you value the position so that you may better negotiate your salary.

There is an additional reason why you simply must ask questions during your job interview. You demonstrate your interest, enthusiasm, and even your competence by the questions you ask. In our discussions with employers, we often hear that the quality of an applicant's questions is every bit as important as the quality of his or her answers in determining whether he or she will be a good fit for the organization.

Most interviewers will be happy to have you pose thoughtful questions throughout the interview. Near the end of the interview, the employer will probably ask whether you have any (other) questions. If you have none, it will probably take you out of the running. But don't ask questions that would have been easily answered if you had prepared appropriately for the interview. And don't ever ask self-serving questions at this point. No questions about pay, vacation or any company benefits! Save these concerns until after you have been offered the job. At this point your questions should deal with your understanding of the organization and its operation. Resist the temptation (or arrogance) to suggest solutions to the interviewer's problems. You will not endear yourself to him or her if he or she has been struggling with these problems for months. You may not fully understand the complexities of this organization and may suggest a solution to a problem that the management team feels is totally inappropriate for their situation. Better to demonstrate your problem solving ability in your past jobs and indicate that once you understand more about their organization you are sure you will be able to work with them to solve problems they may have.

> *You demonstrate your interest, enthusiasm, and even your competence by the questions you ask.*

Chapter 10 presents some of the questions you should always ask if they have not been dealt with earlier in the interview.

YOUR DYNAMISM HELPS SELL YOUR SKILLS

Job candidates usually spend time polishing their verbal skills: how they should respond to questions or what questions they should ask. Yet we know that the nonverbal behaviors speak louder than words. If the applicant verbally says he or she is interested in the company or the position, but his or her nonverbal behavior doesn't indicate any enthusiasm at all, what message does he or she send? Consider that Paul Tsongas, Michael Dukakis, and Bob Dole each lost his bid for the highest job he sought, not because of a lack of qualifications, but largely because each failed to demonstrate dynamism—enough enthusiasm to generate a positive response from the American public.

> *It is not necessarily the most qualified candidate who gets the job, but the most enthusiastic one who demonstrates to the employer what a good fit he or she is for the position.*

You, the job applicant, must be dynamic enough to be credible when you say you are interested in the job. You must be able to look the interviewer in the eye when you describe your accomplishments in order to seem believable. You need to carry yourself with the demeanor of a competent individual and project your voice with the confidence of an individual who has a track record of achievement—of getting things done.

Concentrate on the other person, on the needs of the interviewer and his or her organization. Convey that you are competent and trustworthy through your dynamic interaction with the interviewer. Convey your interest in the interviewer and his or her problems and in your ability to bring your skills and experience to help achieve goals. Remember, it is not necessarily the most qualified candidate who gets the job, but the most enthusiastic one who demonstrates to the employer what a good fit he or she is for the position!

ENGAGE IN A POSITIVE SUMMATION

If this is your initial interview with this firm, don't expect a job offer to be made at this time. Except for lower level positions and some entry-level jobs, expect that you may go through several interviews with the same firm before a decision is made. Just as the employer is likely to take time in considering whether to offer you the position, you too should take time to consider the position. Guard against evaluating a job too soon. There is always time to turn it down later—after an offer has been made. If you decide against a job too soon, you may miss an opportunity at a job that could have been a great fit, or the opportunity to negotiate a mediocre offer into a good one.

Before the interview ends, take an opportunity to summate the job as you understand it and link it to your skills. It is important that you do this both to satisfy yourself that you have a correct and complete understanding of the position as well as to clarify and convey that understanding to the interviewer. Once you obtain the interviewer's agreement as to the scope of the position and the responsibilities of the person in the position, you want to restate your continuing interest in the position and the fit. Whether you simply state that you think you are an excellent match for the position or decide to elaborate a bit on the specific fit should depend on several things:

- how adequately this "fit" was discussed during the interview
- how good a "fit" there actually is (don't belabor this if the fit is not a strong one)
- your reading of the nonverbal cues of the interviewer—if the signals indicate the interviewer wants a rapid close, don't antagonize him or her by being too verbose

No matter the nonverbal cues from the interviewer, do not overdo the close. Once both parties sense the interview is being wrapped up, you must keep your part moving. Make your points, and stress your competence, but do this concisely and keep moving toward the close.

DETERMINE THE NEXT STEP AND FOLLOW-THROUGH

There is one more thing you must do before you leave the interview. Following the summation discussed above, if the employer has not indicated when they expect to make a decision, ASK. Then ask, "If I haven't heard from you by then, may I call to see what my status is?" You will almost always be told to call. This gives you entree for one of your follow-up actions.

If you have not heard from the employer by the date indicated, CALL. If a decision has not yet been made, you have reminded them of your interest and your ability to follow through. Your name and candidacy is on the employer's mind. Be sure to ask the question again, when do they expect a decision, and follow-up with your question again—may you call if you have not heard by then.

If you find that an offer has been made to another candidate, thank them for their interest in you and reaffirm your interest in working with them in the future. At least now you know the outcome and can re-double your efforts with your other job leads.

FOLLOW-UP ACTIONS

Immediately after the interview, write a thank-you letter to the interviewer(s). This is a thoughtful thing to do and it puts your name in front of the employer at an important time—during the decision-making process. This is an opportunity to do more than just thank the person for his or her time. It is an opportunity to remind the interviewer of particular areas which were discussed where there is a particularly good fit between the position and your qualifications. Mention the areas where you can make a significant contribution in as enthusiastic a manner as is both appropriate to the business situation and your personality.

If the hiring decision is to be made yet that day, hand deliver the note to the interviewer's administrative assistant before you leave that same day. Otherwise, post the thank-you later that day. Don't procrastinate. Thank-you letters are time sensitive. Your

---

Client Feedback

"I've learned just how significant a 'thank you' letter can be! A sincere appreciation for the time a person takes to share advice and information with me, has sent little reminders to those individuals to root for my success—translation—refer me to someone who can give me the job I want. I really do believe that the job opportunities that have been coming from 'out of nowhere' are, in part, the result of the 'thank you' letter."

—G.O.

goal is to get your name back in front of the decision maker(s) while they still remember you and before they have made their selection.

There is divided opinion as to whether an interview thank-you note should be handwritten or typewritten (word processed). Some advise the hand written thank-you note since it is more personal. Indeed, if the hiring decision is to be made quickly and you are going to leave a thank-you note with the administrative assistant that same day, you may have no choice but to hand write the note. However, consider that this is a business communication, not a personal letter. A word processed letter is likely to appear more in sync with the business decision to be made. The points you stress, as you cite the fit between the position and your skills, are likely to be clearer to the reader in a word processed letter than in a handwritten one. If your handwriting is difficult to read, then there is no question—you must word process the letter.

Send or drop-off your thank-you letter. Then make sure you make your follow-up calls if you haven't heard from the interviewer by the time indicated.

GREAT ANSWERS TO TOUGH
INTERVIEW QUESTIONS

W hile each interview situation is different, you can expect to be asked certain questions at most job interviews. The questions generally fall into a variety of categories relating to your career goals, motivations, education and training, experiences, accomplishments, and weaknesses, propensity to take initiative, solve problems, and work in team environments, and issues relating to your background and personality.

You also may occasionally encounter illegal and sensitive questions that require tactful responses. You will encounter many different types of interviewers, from the very seasoned and capable to the inexperienced and incompetent. Don't assume all interviewers are the same. Part of your job is to manage the interview to your advantage which means consistently focusing on your capabilities in relationship to the employer's needs.

Some interview questions are historical and background probing in nature while others require you to demonstrate your intelligence in dealing with situations. In all cases, you need to respond in a manner that further demonstrates that you have the five qualities employers are looking for in a face-to-face interview: competence, professionalism, honesty, enthusiasm, and likability.

INTERVIEW TYPES AND STRATEGIES

You are likely to encounter many, if not most, of the questions outlined in this chapter. If, for example, an employer decides to conduct a behavior-based interview, most of the questions may focus on your motivations, accomplishments, and problem-solving capabilities rather than on your personality, education, and work history. In other words, the focus will be on your future capabilities to perform for this employer rather than on your past work history with other employers. Whatever the type of interview you encounter, be prepared to answer each question with thoughtful answers that further demonstrate your competence, professionalism, honesty, enthusiasm, and likability.

When answering any question, keep in mind the importance of **strategy** rather than specific answers to each question. Never try to memorize answers to anticipated questions. If you do, chances are you will sound scripted as well as appear nervous—negatives that may quickly knock you out from further consideration.

Keep in mind the purpose of the first interview is to get invited back to a second interview, and the purpose of the second interview is to get invited back to a third or final interview. Initial interviews usually are not job offer interviews—only one of several interviews in the selection process. In the end, you may be called back for three to five additional interviews—in one case our client returned for 14 interviews—before being selected for a position.

Approach each question with answers that include these characteristics:

1. Positive language
2. Vocal tone of interest and enthusiasm
3. Examples of skills and accomplishments
4. Tactfulness when dealing with sensitive issues
5. Confidence and decisiveness in answering each question

When answering questions, keep the following principles in mind:

1. Listen carefully to the question or statement. Understand exactly what's asked. If you are unsure, ask for clarification.

2. Take time to think through all facts that would be applicable to your response.

3. Use **positive information** to answer directly and to the point. Discuss only the facts relevant to the issue under discussion so that you do not open areas of difficulty. Be truthful, but it is not necessary to offer unsolicited information that could detract from the image you are creating.

4. Seek to focus and re-focus attention on your Success Factors and their related accomplishments. Stress their future use in the position being discussed. Remember that the basic question on the interviewer's mind is: "What can this person do for us?"

5. Consider this response model which is applicable to any interview situation: **skill—application—achievement**. If you apply this model, you will bridge the gap between the questions and your talents, reinforce the validity of your experience, and enhance your level of credibility.

Avoid short "yes" and "no" answers and indecisive responses that may indicate your lack of substance and confidence. Be prepared to give examples or tell short "stories" (one to two minutes each) about what you did and with what consequences. The more examples you can give, the more memorable you will be in the final selection process. While you should answer each question as completely as possible, avoid talking too much. You should be able to answer most questions within 30 seconds to two minutes. Except in cases where you are expected to expand on your answer with examples, answers that go beyond two minutes may indicate you "talk too much"—a real negative in the eyes of many interviewers. If you talk too much now, you'll probably be a bore or chatter box once you're on the job!

ICE BREAKERS THAT SET THE TONE

Often an interviewer may start the interview by throwing out a few open-ended questions that require you to bring some initial structure to the interview. While these questions often catch interviewees off guard and make them nervous, many interviewers still believe these questions are good ice breakers. In fact, interviewers are increasingly criticized by HR professionals for asking such questions, because they yield little useful information for evaluating capabilities; nonetheless, these questions are frequently asked and thus you need to be prepared for them. Remember, the interviewer is not trying to assess your qualifications at this point. He/she may be more concerned with how well you will fit into the organization—the chemistry between the two of you. Be sure you prepare well for this initial question:

> ## Question: Tell me about yourself.

This question may come in other forms, such as "Will you tell me a little about yourself? Can you summarize what you've been doing these past ten years?" Some interviewees never quite "get it" when asked this question. As a result, they quickly lose control of the interview during the critical first five minutes—the time when first impressions count the most and set the tone for the remainder of the interview. Many interviewees never recover from this question, and the interview goes downhill from there! This is not the time to go into a lengthy history or wander off into many different and disconnected directions. Your response should be both focused and purposeful. You should communicate a continuing pattern of interests and skills that relate to the position in question. Here you want to make a favorable first impression that will set the tone for the remainder of the interview. Consider your response to this question as a commercial that sells your services to an employer. The employer is looking for a brief autobiography. You should provide an answer that will include information about where you grew up, where you went to school, your initial work experience, additional education and special training, where you are now, and what you intend to do next. One of the most effective ways to prepare for this question is to develop a 60-second biographic sketch that emphasizes a **pattern** of interests, skills, and accomplishments. Try to focus your response around a common theme related to your major interests and skills. Take, for example, this response which emphasizes computers:

> I was born in Canton, Ohio and attended Lincoln High School. Ever since I was a teenager, I tinkered with **computers**. It was my hobby, my passion, and my way of learning. Like most kids I enjoyed **computer games.**
>
> When my folks gave me a **computer** as a reward for making the honor roll my sophomore year, I mastered DOS, Windows, and WordPerfect within six months. I then went on to teach myself **programming** basics.
>
> By the time I graduated high school, I knew I wanted to study **programming**. From that point on, everything fell in place. My

life revolved around computing. By my junior year at Syracuse, I decided I wanted to work for a major **software** manufacturer. That is why I worked an internship last summer at FastTrack Software.

I now want to work for a major player so I can be at the forefront of breaking trends and **new technology**. When my college roommate told me his cousin, Elizabeth Anne Jones, got her start in your department, I hounded him until he helped me get a referral from Liz, to the employment agency, to you.

I am prepared to answer any questions you may have about my education and experience.

This response sets a nice tone for starting the interview. The interviewee is able to say a lot within 60 seconds by being focused. The message is clear: the interviewee has both passion and focus relating to the position. Emphasizing a pattern, he stays on message and concludes by leaving the door open for additional questions about his education and experience. Unfortunately, some candidates get off on the wrong foot by rambling on for several minutes about their childhood, family, hobbies, travels, and interests. Nothing seems related to a pattern of behavior. Setting the wrong tone with such an unfocused answer, the interview tends to go downhill from there!

Individuals with lots of work experience may have difficulty developing a short and coherent answer to this question. In this case, another way to answer the question is to focus only on your professional experience. You might do this by first seeking clarification with this question directed to the interviewer: "Would you prefer that I discuss my most recent work with XYZ company or would it be most useful to include what I've been doing since graduating from college in 1986?" This question can structure your answer in line with the interviewer's expectations. However, your strongest response will be one that goes beyond the anecdotal. Throughout the interview, you should attempt to communicate a clear pattern of interests, skills, and accomplishments. In the end, the employer wants to **hire your pattern of accomplishments**, if it's appropriate to the company. Once he or she has a clear understanding of your pattern—which hopefully you've identified through Haldane's self-assessment exercise, Success Factor Analysis—you are well on your way to reaching closure with the employer.

REPEAT KEY ACCOMPLISHMENT STATEMENTS

Throughout the interview you will be asked numerous questions about your attitude and ability to do the job. Whenever possible, talk about your accomplishments in terms of what you did and the results of your actions for employers. Give **examples** of your effectiveness which should include specific skills and statistics. In preparation for the interview, develop a series of accomplishment statements in three sentence formats.

Let's assume that the primary requirement for a job is "ability to coordinate." With no more information than that, what are you expected to coordinate? Activities? Data? Information? People? Things? The following three examples will support one individual's capability to prove that she has had experience in **coordinating:**

Opened a new lounge and restaurant within two months after being hired as Director for Clubs for a major government agency. Reviewed existing plan; revised service and product concept; altered interior renovation; coordinated with all individuals having prior input; hired and trained personnel; and monitored quality assurance and financial performance. Results: Operation opened on schedule, within budget; realized successful continuing operation with increased volume while receiving favorable feedback from customers and higher echelons.

Improved the financial status of a multiple retail food service operation for a large hospitality organization. Evaluated existing service and production procedures; studied market, systematized, reorganized and trained personnel; combined functions through attrition; initiated incentives; created promotional goals; *coordinated food service production;* created catering service; prepared budgets and monitored financial performance. Results: Reduced food cost 10%, bar cost 6%, and labor cost 33%; upgraded quality of service while improving employee morale and attendance.

Strengthened management of four large full-service clubs and catering services for a major military establishment. Evaluated and modified programs/services to improve efficiency; developed strategic plan to reduce costs and increase sales; *coordinated better utilization of surplus equipment and supplies;* centralized support functions; enhanced manager's financial awareness by providing a management information tool (software); and motivated personnel through coaching/team building approach. Results: Improved overall financial performance without appropriated fund support; instilled pride in managers which improved sanitation and preparation efforts; reduced employee turnover by 50%; upgraded facilities; and increased sales 31% the first year.

These three examples of effectiveness come from one individual's list of 65 examples of effectiveness that she prepared prior to a job interview. You should be able to produce similar examples of effectiveness to support your primary functional skills. Since you have acquired many functional skills in your work experiences, now you should be able to tell someone about them in a manner they will understand and accept.

CAREER GOALS

Expect to encounter several questions about your career goals. For many interviewees, these are the toughest questions of all because they tend to be open-ended and require the individual to search inside himself or herself for thoughtful answers. If you lack clear career goals, these can be tough questions. If you know your goals, these will be easy questions to answer that also will set the tone for the remainder of the job interview. Indeed, they may help you focus the interview on **your** strengths.

> **Question:** Where do you see yourself five years from now?

Next to the ice breaking "Tell me about yourself" question, this open-ended question is one of the most difficult and stressful ones job seekers face. It often catches them off guard and makes them nervous as they try to come up with a coherent response. If it comes right after the "Tell me about yourself" question, you may feel you've just received a double whammy! It, too, is not a great and informative question but interviewers still use it. The result is often a canned response—"advancing within your organization." If the interviewee really told the truth, he or she would probably say, "I really don't know. I'll see where this job takes me in the next five years!" Employers ostensibly ask this question because they are looking for people who know what they want to do and who are focused on specific professional goals. If you lack goals, you will have difficulty answering this question. If you've developed your resume according to Haldane's principles (*Haldane's Best Resumes For Professionals*), you will have gone through a goal-setting exercise that helps you develop your resume objective. This assessment exercise will help you answer this question. Be sure you arrive at the interview with a clear vision of what you want to do today, tomorrow, and five years from now. Your response should be consistent with the objective on your resume and the skills and accomplishments you're communicating to the interviewer. It should be very employer-centered. In other words, in five years you hope to see yourself working with an employer in an increasingly responsible position, one that enables you to fully utilize your talents and work closely with your colleagues in solving important problems, and one that is very enjoyable; you see yourself taking on many new and exciting challenges that will help you grow professionally. And hopefully this will be with this employer. Do not indicate you hope to start your own business, change careers, or go back to school. Such responses indicate a lack of long-term interest in the employer since you do not plan to stay around long! Some job seekers respond by saying they really hadn't thought that far ahead. While this may be an honest response, the interviewer infers the applicant lacks vision and goals.

> **Question:** How do your career goals today differ from your career goals five years ago?

Your answer to this question will indicate how well formulated or consistent your goals are today compared with the past. Again, the interviewer is looking for patterns and purpose. If, for example, your goals today are the same as five years ago, you may appear to be very focused. On the other hand, if you indicate you had few career goals five years ago but you've learned a great deal in the meantime and now have specific goals, you indicate that you are someone who has learned and improved upon a weakness. If you still have no career goals, you'll appear weak and unfocused to the interviewer.

Question: Describe a major goal you've set for yourself recently.

Give an example of a goal you both set and achieved. Ideally, this should be a professional goal, such as improved your time management practices, achieved new performance targets, or learned a new skill. A personal example can also be appropriate if it reinforces your pattern of accomplishments. For example, if you take a great deal of initiative and quickly move into leadership positions, you might use a personal example relating to your recent community work: organized a community walk-a-thon that raised $30,000 in matching funds to purchase new computers for the local library. Talk about the *results* of achieving your goal. This indicates you set realistic goals and that you focus on outcomes. Select an example that has interesting outcomes related to your efforts. The example should showcase your skills and abilities.

Question: Have you ever thought of switching careers?

Again, the interviewer is looking for patterns and consistency. If you indicate you frequently think about changing careers, you will appear uncertain about yourself and may leave the interviewer wondering when you will next think about making a career change. If you've already made a career change, explain what you did and why and indicate why your current career is the perfect fit for you.

CONVENTIONAL QUESTIONS

You can expect to be asked many additional questions concerning your personality, decision-making style, expectations, experience, work behavior, motivation, education, and skills. If you have been out of school for more than five years, you may not be asked many questions about your education. If you are a recent graduate, you'll probably be asked several standard questions about why you selected a particular school and major, why you did or did not go to college, your grades, subjects you enjoyed the most, your extracurricular activities, leadership roles, work experience, and future educational plans. In lieu of extensive work experience, the interviewer will have to predict future work performance based on your educational experiences. He or she will be especially interested in learning about your career goals and ability to organize, communicate, take initiative, and learn beyond entry-level skills.

Other questions you can expect to encounter in most interviews include the following:

> **Question:** How long have you been looking for a job?

This question touches on your job search competence. If you've been in the job market for a long time, the interviewer might question why you haven't been able to find a job. Is there something wrong with you that other employers noticed? Are you damaged goods? If you are currently employed and looking for employment, you can deal with this question easily—you occasionally look when something interesting comes up. If you're still looking after six months of unemployment, you might indicate that it has taken you a few months to identify what you really want to do. You're just beginning to conduct a comprehensive job search. For example,

> "Since I'm currently employed, I occasionally pursue job leads that look interesting. Only within the last two months have I made a concerted effort to seek new employment. During that time I was invited to eight interviews and was a finalist with three companies. I recently turned down an offer with one company."

Question: Now that you've had a chance to learn more about us, what would you change about our company?

Be careful here. Most companies don't want you to come in and shake up the place—that would be very presumptuous on your part since you know very little about their operations. At the same time, they don't want someone who says "Nothing, everything looks great here." Seek a middle ground by focusing on one or two non-threatening issues that may have come up in your discussions. For example,

"From our discussion of the problem with the southwest accounts, I think we should look into the possibility of consolidating them with the Los Angeles office. However, I think we need to do a thorough cost-benefit analysis of this region before making such a move. We may find it makes more sense to consolidate the LA operations into the Phoenix office."

Such an answer indicates you are open to making changes but you also have a certain non-threatening decision-making style. You sound sensible and you may be innovative.

Question: What would you like to accomplish here in the next five years?

Try to be as specific as possible. Reflect on your previous discussions about the company—its goals, its problems, its priorities. Make sure what you are saying is consistent with the vision of the organization. Focus on the bottom line issues, such as improving ROI, expanding markets by 20 percent, increasing market share by 10 percent, and opening new overseas markets.

> **Question:** What do you find most interesting about this job?

You should focus on the nature of the work, the possible outcomes, the people you'll be working with, the knowledge and skills you will both use and gain, and your long-term interests.

> **Question:** What do you do if your ideas are rejected?

Indicate that you are not a quitter or someone who gets discouraged by rejections. You'll continue to sell your ideas as long as your bosses are open to new ideas. Try to give an example of how an idea that was initially rejected was later accepted because of your persistence and change in presentation. You might end with posing a related question to the interviewer: "How does your company encourage ideas from its employees? Does it reward those who contribute useful ideas?" These questions will give you an idea of the company's management and communication styles.

> **Question:** Have you ever worked with a difficult boss?

If your answer is "yes," indicate how you best dealt with the situation. Were there certain things you did that kept you motivated and productive despite some of the negative aspects of the relationship?

> **Question:** What makes you angry?

Avoid saying "Nothing"—no one will believe you. Show some passion here for what you really value in people, work, and companies. The best answer to this question, and one that stays on message, is this: "Not getting the work done according to expectations!" However, consider other options, such as "People who only think of themselves rather than others and the company's goals," "Dishonest and devious people," "A company that lies to its employees," or "Injustice."

Question: How would you rate your last employer?

Be careful not to say negative things about your previous employer, even though you may feel it's justified. Candidates who speak negatively about other people in a job interview tend to have a serious attitude problem which employers are not interested in hiring. Commit sins of omission by focusing on your last employer's positives. Let this employer also know you have high expectations for your new employer. For example, your previous employer may have been very good at mentoring, providing training opportunities, involving you in the decision-making process, and letting you take on new responsibilities. The fact that he was a poor manager, occasionally treated you unfairly, or engaged in sexual harassment should not be mentioned here. Let the interviewer know what you really liked about that job and employer. If asked to rate the employer on a scale of 1 to 10, be honest by giving him high scores on his positives.

Question: How would your current supervisor rate your performance?

This is not the time to confess any difficulties with your supervisor. Focus on your positives since most supervisors will give their subordinates positive recommendations. Fear of lawsuits and professional courtesy (he or she needs to "move on" with his or her career) often prevent supervisors from giving frank evaluations of their subordinates to strangers. Few will volunteer negative comments, even though you may feel they will talk about some problems you've had on the job. For example,

> "Mr. Wells will most likely tell you that I am an exceptional employee who regularly exceeds his goals. I've been very successful in negotiating new contracts with our overseas suppliers."

> ## Question: How might your subordinates rate you as a supervisor?

Again, focus on the positives. Select two or three words that best describe your relationship with your subordinates and then briefly elaborate on that relationship. If, for example, you are known for being "fair" and "open" with them, focus on these defining characteristics:

> "Most would tell you that I've always been fair and open with them. We insist on sharing both the responsibilities and rewards of our work. I'm an especially good listener who tries to be as responsive as possible to their needs, both professional and personal. We have a wonderful team atmosphere that has been extremely productive for the company."

> ## Question: What would your colleagues say about you?

Since employers are looking for "chemistry," it's important that you convey your ability to work well with others. Focus on those elements of your relationship that communicate your ability to work well with colleagues. Give examples if at all possible:

> "I'm very well respected by my colleagues. They often turn to me for advice and leadership. In fact, when I first joined ABC Company, relations with colleagues were severely strained due to several personality conflicts. Everyone seemed busy at work, but no one talked to each other or smiled. I thought perhaps I made a mistake in taking the job since it was not an enjoyable place to work. However, within six weeks I saw a dramatic change in the atmosphere. People actually started talking with each other! I'm generally a very happy and out-going person who loves to schmooze but with a clear purpose in mind—getting the job done. I decided to meet everyone and ask their advice on several key issues. I was surprised with the response. As both my supervisor and colleagues will testify, the change was largely due to my presence and efforts to develop a team approach in our division. My division within ABC Company is now one of

the most dynamic within the company. It's known for its bright and innovative team. I'm proud to have been partly responsible for this change. They're really great people to work with."

> **Question:** We all have weaknesses. What are some of your major weaknesses?

This is not the time to confess all your problems nor to confidently say you have no weaknesses. The best way to handle this question is to mention personal weaknesses that are outside the job or a professional weakness that you have already improved upon. For example, you might say:

"I have a real weakness for chocolate that tends to go right to my waist! I'm watching my calories very carefully these days."

"I've never been good with accounting. I'm glad this job doesn't involve accounting!"

"I used to have difficulty following-up on my marketing calls. Once I started using this new contact manager program, I've been able to greatly improve my productivity. In fact, I'm not sure how I lived without it for so long!"

> **Question:** What type of people do you find most difficult to work with?

You should indicate that you manage to get along with most people, however difficult they may be. Note that you sometimes encounter difficult people, but you manage to successfully work through differences. If you can, give an example of a difficult person you managed to get along with that might also emphasize your people management skills. Keep your answer positive. Avoid the temptation of communicating negative attitudes toward others, however difficult they may be.

> **Question:** What types of decisions do you prefer not to make?

Show that you are generally decisive but mention that there are situations that give you time to pause or you are learning how to better make decisions. For example, "I sometimes have difficulty choosing between two equally good ideas" or "I used to have difficulty saying 'No' to people until I learned how to better set priorities."

> **Question:** How truthful and honest do you consider yourself?

This is the time to share your philosophy on people and work. Let the interviewer know how much you value truthfulness and honesty in relationships. If you can, give an example of how these values have played an important part in your work and life. This also is a good time to expand on these values and address the whole issue of communications in the workplace—how important it is to have clear lines of communication and honest feedback on a regular basis. You might even raise some questions about the company's performance appraisal system. How does it work?

> **Question:** Ideally, what type of job are you really looking for?

Your answer should directly relate to the position in question. However, you also may want to expand upon it by indicating your long-term career interest with the company. You would hope to move to other positions within the next five years. At this point, ask about the normal progression within the company for someone with your skills and experience. If all goes well, where would they expect you to be five years from now? What type of job would they like to see you in?

Question: What is your biggest failure?

Focus on something outside your work or something that happened on the job that you later fixed. For example,

> "My biggest failure was not being selected as a SEAL because I was diagnosed with night vision problems. When I was 18, all I wanted to be was a SEAL. But I'm glad I didn't, because I may have overlooked this exciting career in information technology."

> "When I was working at CL Advertising Associates, I lost the $10 million Jettler account after only six weeks on the job! I really felt bad—thought I would be fired. I was determined to get the account back, and I did it within six months. Today the account generates $25 million in sales and makes up one-third of CL Advertising Associates accounts. For that I won the 'Best Employee of the Year' award!"

Question: What's the worst day you've ever had and how did you deal with it?

It's time to play hero. Pick an example of a bad day in which you came to the rescue. An ideal bad day is one in which a problem was created by someone else—the boss, a colleague, or a customer—and you came in and solved it in a very innovative and decisive manner.

Question: Why were you fired?

This is not the time and place to go into all the details and point fingers at others about your firing. If you've been fired, accept it as a fact of life and move on. Put your firing into a larger perspective. For example,

> "The job was eliminated because of the lack of work."

"We decided to part company over some important strategic and ethical issues. My former employer has asked that I not discuss these issues with others since they are proprietary."

"My skills were no longer needed."

"We decided it was time that I moved on to a more challenging position."

Question: Why did you quit that job?

Be honest but don't be stupid by dragging up all the negative aspects of the job that may have motivated you to leave. Like being fired, you need to put this job behind you and move ahead. In most situations, the following responses would be appropriate even though they may cover up a lot of difficult relationships:

"Since it was a dead end job, I felt it was time to move on in my career."

"It was not the right fit for my interests and skills."

"I was approached with an opportunity I couldn't refuse."

Question: How long would you expect to stay with our company?

The answer to this question should be obvious—"As long as I enjoy what I'm doing and am growing professionally." If you have a work history of changing jobs frequently, you may need to deal with that issue up front. For example, if the interviewer notices that on average you change jobs every two to three years, he's probably trying to get some indication if you plan to repeat this job-hopping pattern. Anticipating this potential objection to hiring you, you might respond as follows:

"I'm really looking for a long-term commitment with a company where I can fully utilize my skills and grow professionally.

In the past, most of my jobs were entry-level positions with small companies that did not offer many opportunities after a year or two. I've purposefully decided not to pursue opportunities with such companies again."

If you are indeed a job hopper who gets restless after a year or two on the job, you need to deal with this issue in a different manner. Ideally, you recognize this is a problem and you've made the necessary adjustments so that you've hopefully broken the pattern:

"My previous jobs where not good fits because I was uncertain what I really wanted to do with my life. I often took jobs that looked interesting but in reality were not compatible with my motivations and skills. I've had a long talk with myself, as well as a career counselor, which helped me better focus on what I really should be doing given my interests, skills, accomplishments, and goals. I see this job as a perfect fit for what I really want to do for at least the next five years."

Question: What are your salary expectations?

If this question arises early in the interview, try to move it toward the end of the interview, after you've been offered the job. The reason is simple: you need to know more about the position, and the employer needs to know more about you before the both of you can value you. If you prematurely state a salary figure, you may eliminate yourself from future consideration or price yourself too low. Everything you do and say during the interview should be aimed at increasing your value in the eyes of the employer. When you get to the job offer, both of you should be well prepared to talk about salary. You should know exactly what the position is worth, given your previous salary research and information you acquired about the position. Now you are prepared to negotiate salary and benefits. When the question is raised by the interviewer, respond by turning the question around: "How much do you normally pay for someone with my qualifications?" Try to get the employer to reveal his hand first. You want to establish a salary range within which you can negotiate. For example, if the employer responds by saying "We normally pay in the range of $70,000 to $80,000," put the employer's high figure at the bottom of your range so you have common ground from which to negotiate: "I was thinking more in line with $80,000 to $90,000." Chances are you can negotiate a final salary somewhere in the $80's.

Question: Are you willing to take a cut in pay to join our company?

Be careful in answering this question. It opens the whole salary issue which you should focus on when you have been offered the job. If you say "yes," you may lock yourself into a bad salary negotiation situation. You have several options, from the lighthearted to the serious; we prefer the final response:

> "This is not the direction I was planning to take with my career. We obviously need to talk about your compensation package."

> "Do you make the same offer to other candidates?"

> "Do you plan to reduce your salary when I come on board?"

> "Let's talk more about the position so I have a better idea of what it's really worth. I'm very open to discussing stock options, incentivized pay, and other forms of compensation in lieu of salary. Can you tell me more about the responsibilities and how you measure performance? Perhaps you could also outline your compensation package."

Question: What do you see as your major strengths for this job?

Select three of your major qualities that you know are desired by the employer. Explain to the employer how your goals, skills, and accomplishments seem to be a perfect match for this job.

> **Question:** How important is job security?

Your answer should indicate that you expect your job security to be linked to your performance. Also, use this question as an opportunity to acquire more information on how the company's performance appraisal system operates and how well the previous occupant of the position performed:

> "Since I've never really had job security, it really hasn't been important to me. I've always expected my job tenure would be tied to my performance. I also expect a company will reciprocate by setting clear performance goals and regularly evaluating performance. Could you explain how the performance appraisal system operates here at ABC Company? Also, what has been the average tenure of someone in this position? Could you tell me a little more about the previous person who held this position—his or her strengths and weaknesses?"

> **Question:** What are the major reasons for your success?

This is not the time to become extremely self-centered and arrogant. Keep in mind that employers are often looking for team players rather than Lone Rangers. A good response to this question may relate to a mentor and/or philosophy of work or the people you work with. Also, use this question as an opportunity to inquire about an appropriate "fit for success" with this company. For example,

> "Many years ago I learned an important lesson from Bob Nelson, who was my first supervisor and really became my most important mentor. One day he told me his secret to success: 'Look at each day as a new opportunity to be your very best. Set high goals, be honest, never say no, and work with people who share your passion for doing their best.' I've always remembered that bit of advice and try to live it every day. As Bob would tell you, I'm very self motivated, tenacious, and honest. I really love what I do and surround myself with people who share similar pas-

sions. I really thrive in such an environment. Is this the type of environment I'm likely to find here at ABC Company? Can you tell me a little more about the characteristics of successful people in your company? What do you see as some of the key success factors for this position?"

Question: Why should we hire you?

Give a one to two-minute summary presentation on why you are the perfect candidate. Talk about how your goals are the same as the company's goals; what demonstrated skills you have that are needed by the company; and how your past pattern of accomplishments will likely continue with this company. Finally, stress that you think this will be a great place to work and do so with enthusiasm. Let the employer know you really want the job.

Question: What do you do to improve your knowledge and skills in this field?

Focus on what additional training and learning you acquire on a regular basic. Employers want self-starters who understand the importance to being self-motivated and constantly up-to-date in their skills.

Question: What attracted you most to this position?

Focus your answer on the most attractive qualities—the company, the customers, the product, the challenge, and/or the ability to fully use your skills. Show enthusiasm as you answer this question. Let the employer know you really want the job.

Question: What is your management style?

Your answer should be in line with the organization's management style. Be sure you've researched this aspect of the organization prior to the interview. Know if this is a hierarchical, team-oriented, or flat organization. If you are a command and control type entering a team-oriented organization, chances are you will be operating in a foreign culture.

> **Question:** How much time do you think it will take before you will be up and running in this position?

Ask for clarification about expectations. For example, will you go through an initial training period? Will you be setting initial performance goals with your boss? Who will you be working with at first? What responsibilities will you initially be given? When are you expected to begin operating solo? Based on responses to these questions, indicate to the interviewer that you expect to be fully prepared within the expected time period.

> **Question:** What two things would you like to improve about yourself in the coming year?

Be careful with this question. This is another way to get at your weaknesses. It's not necessary to confess your shortcomings here or note your professional problems. Focus on something that is either irrelevant or tangential to the job, such as improving your golf score, losing ten pounds, doing more volunteer work, or acquiring a new skill such as public speaking.

> **Question:** You appear overqualified for this job. Why should I hire you?

If you are truly overqualified for the job, you may want to pass on it. Accepting a job that is beneath your qualifications will probably lead to dissatisfaction with the job. On the other hand, if you really want the job, outline why this job is so special to you. Show a great deal of enthusiasm in letting the employer know that this job really is the perfect fit for you; it's something you will really love doing.

> **Question:** We're considering two other candidates for this position. What is so special about you? Why should we hire you rather than someone else?

Don't be distracted by the mention of two other candidates since you don't know anything about them and they could be fictitious. Focus on what strengths you bring to the table. These should be consistent with the four things most employers are looking for in candidates during the job interview: competence, professionalism, enthusiasm, and likability. Remember, they are looking for chemistry between you and them. Be prepared to summarize in 60 seconds why you are the best candidate for the job. Also, let the employer know you want the job and you will enjoy working with them. A lack of interest in the job may indicate a lack of enthusiasm for the job and them.

> **Question:** Do you have any regrets?

Be careful not to confess your weaknesses with this question. Focus any regrets on lost opportunities, such as "I wish I would have moved to this city five years earlier," "I wish I would have completed my MBA right after leaving the Army," or "I wish I had learned about your company and applied for this position earlier."

Alternatively, "No, I have no regrets. I always focus on the future and treat the past as an important learning experience."

> **Question:** What things give you the greatest satisfaction?

Assuming you've identified many of your accomplishments (those things you do well and enjoy doing), this should be an easy question to answer. Focus on employer-oriented or job-related experiences, such as "Seeing the results of my work," "Putting together projects that make a difference in people's lives," or "Finding cost-effective solutions to a very difficult problem."

Question: How do you spend your free time?

This question may have several purposes. The interviewer may be just curious about your personal life without getting into illegal questions. He may also want to know how well rounded you are in your personal and professional lives. Focus on some of the standard hobbies or activities most people engage in—tennis, golf, boating, reading, music, opera, collecting, gardening, or cooking. If you are operating a home-based business as a sideline, you may not want to reveal your entrepreneurial spirit—it may indicate you are planning to leave and go solo as soon as the business starts doing well. If you are into extreme sports, such as sky diving, bungee jumping, and mountain climbing, you may want to keep these to yourself for the time being.

Question: How much time do you spend on the Internet each week?

You may want to distinguish between personal and professional time on the Internet. If your current or previous job required using the Internet, explain what positive roles it played in your job. On the personal side, be careful how you answer this question. Spending lots of time on the Internet communicating with your family may be seen as a negative.

Question: What kinds of Internet sites do you most frequently visit?

Mention sites that indicate you are someone with substantive interests or someone with an unusual hobby that makes you unique, such as collecting 18th century compasses. This may lead to a very interesting conversation that further emphasizes your likability.

Question: How do you handle criticism?

This question looks for indicators of your decision-making style, how you handle stress, how receptive you are to others, and your responses to feedback. Indicate that you are open-minded and take all criticism seriously, but you also consider the source. Explain that you deal with criticism in a professional, rather than personal, manner. You talk with the person to better understand the reason for the criticism. If it's valid, you make the necessary changes. If not, you explain the situation to the critic. If you are seldom a subject of criticism, indicate that to the interviewer: "I am seldom criticized for my work. But if I were to be criticized, I would . . ."

> **Question:** What did you like the most and the least about your previous jobs?

Be careful not to bad mouth your previous employers. Focus on your strengths and weaknesses in relationship to the job fit. If, for example, you were in a job that required accounting skills and this is not a skill you enjoyed using, indicate this as one of the things you least liked about your previous jobs. Before going into the interview, make a list of things you both loved and disliked about your previous jobs. Focus on the nature of the work and the skills involved rather than the individuals and personalities involved. In many cases, the worst part of a job involves the people you must work with. This is not the time nor place to reveal the fact that you had "people problems" in your previous jobs. Hopefully, with a new mix of people, these problems will not recur in the next job. Focus most of your answer on those things you really enjoyed doing. Give examples of your skills and accomplishments.

BEHAVIOR-BASED QUESTIONS

More and more employers are beginning to ask different types of questions that go beyond conventional job interview questions about education, goals, personality, motivations, and work history. These questions focus on the individual's behavior and core competencies. As employers better define positions in terms of core competencies, they ask different types of questions that enable them to assess a candidate's ability to do the job. The behavioral questions are designed to better predict individual performance. Most such questions are open-ended and require the interviewee to provide examples of his or her accomplishments. Individuals who do well in these types of interviews are individuals who have a large reservoir of accomplishments from which to draw.

Haldane's job search methods are ideally suited for behavioral-based interviews. Our clients go through a thorough self-assessment process that emphasizes skills and accomplishments. Through Success Factor Analysis individuals identify their motivated skills and abilities. They learn to talk about their strengths as a pattern of accomplishments. When faced with behavioral-based interview questions, they are prepared to give examples that validate their patterns of accomplishments. This assessment technique is outlined in the companion volume, *Haldane's Best Resumes For Professionals.*

Behavioral questions usually come in two different forms: self-appraisal questions and situational "What if..." questions. If you encounter any of the following questions, you're probably interviewing with someone who is trying to analyze your pattern of behavior. Be prepared to share lots of examples of your accomplishments.

> **Question:** Tell me about something you recently took responsibility for that was outside your job description.

In answering this question, you should be demonstrating your initiative, team spirit, and sense of ownership with the company. Select an example that stresses these skills and your orientation toward the workplace.

> **Question:** Can you give me a recent example of how you dealt with a particularly difficult employee?

The question focuses on your supervisory style and how you handle potentially volatile situations. You need to give an example that shows you can handle such situations with ease. However, the next question allows you to take corrective actions that could alter the outcomes.

Question: If you had to do it over, what would you do differently?

This question is used a lot for following up on examples of behavior. Here you need to demonstrate that you do entertain alternative approaches, you listen, and you make changes if necessary. Avoid communicating an inflexible decision-making style which probably indicates you are headed for trouble.

Question: Why would you do that?

This probing follow-up question looks at motivation and the decision-making process. Be prepared to give three good reasons (three is always a good number to enumerate) for your decision.

Question: If you discovered an employee was sharing trade secrets with the competition, what would you do?

Question: If an employee reported being harassed by another employee, how would you handle the situation?

Question: If one of your clients calls and informs you that his company is taking his business elsewhere, how would you respond?

Question: If you learned that XYZ Company was moving into our Canadian market by acquiring Seatram Corporation, what would you do?

Question: If you needed to create three new positions in your expanding division, what three positions would you choose?

Question: If you had to downsize by three positions, which three positions would go first?

All of these "What if..." questions require creative responses that provide evidence of your intelligence, decision-making capabilities, organizational and people management skills, and street savvy. Your answers may tell the interviewer a great deal about how quickly you think on your feet and how you are likely to behave in many critical and stressful situations.

Employers who ask behavior questions in job interviews also are likely to ask similar questions when checking references. For example, rather than just verify employment dates, duties, and salary history or ask general "Tell me about . . ." questions, behavior questions asked of references can be very specific and focus on identifying an individual's patterns of behavior:

"What were his three major achievements this past year?"

"Can you give me an example of how he solved customer service problems?"

"What were some of her major weaknesses she corrected?"

"If you hired her again, what two changes would you like to see her make?"

"What five words might best predict his future performance?"

Some questions may combine conventional and behavioral questions. For example,

Question: Do you prefer working on your own or as part of a team?

This question is often asked by an interviewer who is looking for someone with a team orientation. If the response is "part of the team," a likely follow-up behavior question would be this:

> **Question:** Can you give me a recent example of your
> successful team work experience?

It's more difficult to prepare for behavior questions than for the more conventional interview questions. Behavior questions tend to be open-ended and require creative responses tied to specific examples and stories of success. However, you can anticipate many of the questions and develop a strategy for responding to them. Focus on your major accomplishments, especially those that demonstrate major skills and patterns of behavior. Be prepared to give lots of examples of how you made decisions, why you did what you did, and what you might do differently. These can be stressful questions, especially if you come prepared with answers to the more conventional anticipated questions. While the employer may not be expecting specific answers to these questions, he or she will be able to detect how intelligently and tactfully you deal with situations that are important to the company. He or she will be able to predict to some degree how well you may fit into the company culture. These questions really do get at the heart of determining "chemistry" between you and the employer.

SENSITIVE, ILLEGAL, AND STUPID QUESTIONS

Despite warnings to the contrary, many employers still ask illegal questions or ones that border on being illegal. Many of these questions deal with age, family responsibilities, and lifestyle. If you encounter such questions, you need to be prepared to respond. Some interviewers may be shocked or feel insulted and respond negatively. Others deal with the questions with a combination of humor and honesty. You have to decide how best to respond to such questions. Some interviewees actually volunteer information that would be considered illegal to acquire through questions. They often do this when asked the ice-breaker question, "Tell me about yourself." They may start by saying they are 29 years old, happily married, two children, a church-going Catholic, and a liberal Democrat. Having said that, there's not much more the interviewer can ask that's considered illegal!

Assuming you will not volunteer such information, you need to be prepared to handle these sensitive questions. Do not be afraid to inject humor into your replies; it can sometimes relax the formality of the situation. Also, don't be afraid of a little confrontation, especially when you know you are correct. You might respond:

"That's a (great) (strange) (different) question. No one has ever asked me that before. Why did you?"

You are attempting to determine why the interviewer is asking such a question. If you know why, then you can reply with an appropriate answer. Most often the interviewer will let it drop and move on to a reasonable question.

Here are some of the many potentially illegal and sensitive questions you might encounter:

1. Are you able to work overtime, evenings and weekends?

2. How do you feel about attending conferences with (men) (women)?

3. What child care arrangements have you made?

4. What type of position does your spouse have?

5. Do you think that you can supervise (men) (women), and how do you think (men) (women) will react to you?

6. This job has always been handled by a (female) (male). Do you think you can handle it?

7. Are you willing to put career interests before self-interests?

Case In Point

I had a client who was being interviewed for a plant manager position. Part of the process was being interviewed by some of the workers he would supervise. One woman, a line worker, asked him "What if I am having my period and come into your office and start chewing your ass. What would you do?"

What helped him win the position was when he said that he understands that everyone had "bad" days, for whatever reason, and he expects everyone to treat everyone with civility and respect, himself included. If she did this to anyone, he would have her come back when she was more composed.

Case In Point

At an automotive manufacturing company, several of our candidates have been interviewed seated at the center of the board room table, with the HR manager at one end of the table, the hiring manager at the other, and several other employees opposite, in a U-shaped panel arrangement.

The HR manager begins: "We're so happy to have you here with us today. We just want you to relax and be yourself and help us all get acquainted with you. We're really very informal here. To help put you at ease, we're just going to go around the table and introduce ourselves. I'm Alice Anderson, and I'm the Human Resources director. I'm 42 and I've been with the company for 10 years now. I'm married, my husband is a salesman for Proctor and Gamble; we have two children and a couple of dogs, and live in Pleasantville. Off the job I really enjoy gardening and crafts, and our family attends Beth Synagogue."

Then, proceeding in order around the table: "Hi, I'm Bill Bologna. I'm 49 and I've been a production manager here for about 8 years now. My professional focus is on ISO-9000 implementation. I'm divorced and have joint custody of our 3 children with my wife, who lives in Upperville. I play softball with the company team, and I'm active at First Christian Church."

"Hi, my name is Chuck Charles. I'm in the purchasing department and I've been with the company now for 7 years. I'm gay and my partner and I live in Lowertown in a 100-year-old house that I'm remodeling in my spare time. I'm quite active in the AIDS ministry at the Community Life Church; and here at work, I've been an organizer for United Way for the past few years."

"Good afternoon. My name is Doris Darling. I'm 37 and single, and living with my elderly parents in Upperville. I work in the accounting office and I've been with the company for 12 years now. I get around more than you might guess from the wheelchair that I'm in. I enjoy travelling and I've been from coast to coast, since I breed dachshunds and show them at AKC events. I'm not a joiner so I'm not in any clubs, but I enjoy spending time with my friends."

"Hello, let me introduce myself. I'm Edgar Eager and I'm the manager of the marketing department where the open position will be based. I've been in the department for 4 years; and before that I was in sales for 6 years. I'm married; and my wife and I have one son of our own and two daughters from my previous marriage, who live with us. I'm just about to hit the big four-o, so as you can imagine, I've been getting a lot of ribbing about that lately. I'm very involved in my children's activities, including sports and music; and my wife and I are both on a bowling team."

"There, now you know us. Why don't you tell us about yourself...??"

At this point, it was only because of thorough preparation that our clients gave strictly functional details about themselves, not age, religion, gender preference, marital status, etc.

8. What are your computer skills? Would you be interested in doing some word processing?

9. How do you feel about women's liberation?

10. By the way, would you mind telling me: "Just how old are you?"

11. How do you respond to authority?

12. How do you define sexual harassment?

13. Where were you born?

14. What's your nationality?

15. Are you married, divorced, separated, or single?

16. Are you living with anyone?

17. What holidays do you celebrate?

18. Do you have any disabilities that affect your work?

19. What is your health situation like?

20. Have you ever been arrested?

21. Are you on any medications?

22. Do you ever abuse alcohol or drugs?

Case in Point

One client attended an interview, only to be asked what her husband does for a living; a question that had no relevance to the position, and yet really didn't warrant the angry response she gave. She said angrily "You can't ask me that; it's an illegal question!", and then proceeded to storm out of the interview. In our follow-up meeting, I asked this client if she wanted the job? Her reply was "yes, it would be a perfect match, but he shouldn't have asked me such a question." I tell my clients that interviewers ask these questions to see what your response might be. They don't care about the facts. They are only testing you to see if you'll get angry, and how you'll react in a difficult situation. If you get angry, that interviewer "got" you. Now decide whether this question is worth losing the job over. If it is, you probably wouldn't be happy in that environment anyway.

23. How many children do you have?

24. What church do you attend?

25. How do you think my older employees would react if I hired you?

26. Do you have many debts?

27. Do you own or rent your home?

28. How much insurance do you have?

29. How much do you weigh?

30. Do you plan to have any more children?

31. What does your spouse think about your career?

32. Have you ever brought a law suit against an employer?

33. Have you ever filed for workers' comp?

34. Where do you usually go on vacation?

35. What do you think about romance in the office?

36. Have you ever been sexually harassed?

37. Do you have plans to get married?

38. Tell me about your family.

9

QUESTIONS YOU SHOULD
ALWAYS ASK

N ow it's your turn. You need to know if this will be a great
place to work. You can't find this out unless you ask lots of
questions about the nature of the work, the company, and the
people you'll be working with.

Answering employers' questions is only one aspect of the job interview. Asking questions of the interviewer is equally important. In fact,
many employers report selecting candidates who ask the best questions.
It's the quality of the interviewee's questions that really impressed them—
more so than their specific answers to questions.

GATHERING INFORMATION

Remember, the interview should be a two-way street. Both you and
the employer need more information about each other before you can
make intelligent decisions. While you may have done extensive pre-in-
terview research on the company and employer, you now need to ask
several questions during the interview. In addition to gathering important information, the mere act of asking questions indicates you are
interested in the employer. You should never be caught asking this killer
question: "What do you do here?" This question indicates you haven't
done your homework and thus you have little interest in this employer.
Ask this question at the beginning of the interview and the rest of the
interview will probably be downhill from there!

It's surprising how interviewees respond to this final interview question: "Do you have any questions?" Many interviewees say "No, I think
everything is clear" and get up and leave. Such a response indicates one
of three things. First, the interviewee shows little interest in the employer. Second, the interviewee lacks sufficient knowledge and experi-

ence to ask questions about the job and company. Third, the interviewee is anxious to leave this stressful situation!

If you come to the interview prepared to only answer questions, you may raise more questions in the mind of the interviewer about your interests, motivations, and experience. In fact, you should be asking questions throughout the interview. In many cases, your questions should seek clarification to the interviewer's questions, redirect sensitive questions, and follow-up on important issues. For example, if you are asked "What are your salary requirements?" you might turn this question around by asking another related question which places you in a more advantageous position (you want the employer to reveal his hand first on this issue): "What do you normally pay for someone with my qualifications?" If asked about your management style, explain your style but end with an informational question: "Is the style I've outlined an effective one for this company?" If asked about solving a hypothetical problem, ask "Is this a problem here?" If asked an illegal question such as "Are you married, divorced, separated, or single?" you might respond with this sobering question: "Is my marital status important to this job?"

> *You'll be communicating some of the most important qualities employers are looking for in candidates— competence, professionalism, enthusiasm, and likability.*

The old adage that 50 percent of an answer is contained in how you formulate the question is especially relevant to the job interview. Be prepared to ask thoughtful questions throughout the job interview. The very act of injecting your questions during the interview will keep the interview lively, focused, interesting, and informative. You'll be seen as an engaging personality who can hold his own in what is a seemingly stressful situation. Best of all, you'll be communicating some of the most important qualities employers are looking for in candidates—competence, professionalism, enthusiasm, and likability. Indeed, when you leave the interview, you want the interviewer to say, "I like her. She's bright and enthusiastic. She asked some really good questions. Let's invite her back."

THINGS YOU NEED TO KNOW

As many people will testify, the job they thought they interviewed for was not the one they ended up with. Something strange happened between the interview and the first 12 months on the job. In many cases, what happened is simple: the individual failed to ask enough questions about the job and company. What appeared interesting on paper ended up being much more complex. Indeed, three months into the job they often discover the company is not stable nor growing, advancement opportunities are limited, the management style is archaic, individual initiative is not encouraged, work is stressful, the organization culture is

> *There are certain sensitive questions you should avoid asking, such as anything relating to salary and benefits.*

sick, there's lots of debilitating internal politics, people don't talk to each other, and the boss is a real jerk! The so-called great new job has quickly lost its luster. And the future does not look good. You probably made a mistake and should consider updating your resume and start looking for greener pastures.

Had you asked the right questions, chances are such organizational realities would have been more apparent prior to accepting the position. Did you, for example, ask about the companies financial health? Did you inquire about the management style? Did you ask to speak with the people you would be working with, including your boss, co-workers, and subordinates? Did you ask about employee turnover rates and how others liked working for this company? If you failed to ask many of these basic questions, chances are you may be in for some on-the-job surprises!

TYPES OF QUESTIONS TO ASK

Before going to a job interview, prepare a list of questions you would like to ask the interviewer. Keep in mind that there are certain sensitive questions you should avoid asking, such as anything relating to salary and benefits. If you raise these questions early in the interview, you will most likely be seen throughout the interview as someone who is primarily interested in compensation. You'll never recover from such inappropriate questions. These questions should be raised but only at the very last interview—when you are offered the job.

Most of your questions should fall into these five major categories:

1 Questions about jobs and careers

2. Questions about the company

3. Questions about the industry

4. Questions about the selection process

5. Questions about compensation

QUESTIONS ABOUT JOBS AND CAREERS

Assuming you've done your research about the position prior to the interview, you should generally know what's involved in doing the job. However, the content of a job will differ from one organization to another. You need to ask questions about the position in order to get a better understanding of the scope of work, duties and responsibilities, relationships with others, and anticipated problems. The position description will give you an initial idea of the formal duties and responsibilities. But it doesn't really get into the overall dynamics of working in the position. Consequently, you need to ask several of these questions to get a better idea of what it's really like doing the work:

Question: Can you tell me more about the position?

This is a good open-ended question, similar to the interviewer's "Tell me about yourself" question. Listen carefully for any clues about potential problems. While the interviewer may take this question as an opportunity to sell you on the position, you want to probe for realities relating to the work. Ask several follow-up questions relating to responsibilities, expectations, reporting procedures, performance goals, evaluation, potential problems.

Question: How important is this position to the organization?

You may discover this is a very critical position and thus the company attaches a great deal of value to it—which should show up during your salary negotiation session!

Question: Why is this position open?

Good question to ask because it should reveal certain expectations. If it's a new position, it's probably not well defined because it hasn't been operational. If you're coming into a new position, you may have a lot of latitude to develop it along the lines of your strengths. If it's a well-established position, there may be certain expectations about how you must adapt to the position. You also may uncover a high turnover rate with the position which may indicate some inherent problem with how the position is structured vis-a-vis other positions in the company.

Question: Is this a new position?

New positions are double-edged swords. They can offer great opportunities for initiative and innovation. You can prove your value by producing new and expected results. At the same time, these can be dangerous positions. Expectations may be unrealistic. Workloads may become onerous. And in the end, the position may be abolished because it doesn't work out. Know what you're getting into before accepting such a position.

Question: What happened to the last person in this position?

You need to know if you are coming into a difficult or routine situation. Remember, employers have certain expectations for a position based upon the work of previous individuals in that position. The expectations could be unrealistic and thus a basis for the last person leaving the position. If the person was a high performer, you'll be coming into a situation with very high expectations about your performance. You'll be compared to the previous occupant. If the person was controversial or a problem, you may be entering a situation where the expectations are uncertain or conflicting.

> **Question:** If she were promoted, what position did she move to?

The answer to this question will give you an idea about advancement opportunities within the organization. Try to find out if this is the normal progression pattern for this position. However, if no one moves up in the organization from this position, this may be an indication that you're interviewing for a dead end position.

> **Question:** Could I talk to her about her work here?

If the answer is "Certainly," you're probably dealing with a very open organization which has nothing to hide. However, should the interviewer be hesitant or qualify the "yes," this may be an indication of some trouble with either the position or the person.

> **Question:** If fired, what were some of her problems?

Here you'll be able to get a good idea of the expectations, both positive and negative, for the position. You might want to follow-up with some clarification questions, such as "Was this more a problem of her qualifications, personality, or the situation?" or "What might you have done differently to avoid this problem?"

> **Question:** How long do most people stay in this position?

Get some indication of tenure. Is this position, for example, considered a stepping-stone to other positions? How long do you need to demonstrate your performance before moving on in the organization? Is advancement relatively rapid or slow?

Question: Who will I be working with? Can you tell me something about them?

At least during the final interviews, you should be able to identify as well as meet the individuals you will be working with. Start with an organizational chart to identify where this position fits into the larger scheme of positions within the organization. What are their professional backgrounds? How long have they been around? Who's the real star of the group? Do the people you meet give you an immediate favorable impression? Do you think you'll like working with them? Do they seem collegial? Schmooze a little to get some sense of their interpersonal temperaments. Your immediate gut reaction may say a lot about whether or not you'll enjoy working with these people.

Question: How will my performance be evaluated?

A professional organization regularly evaluates its employees and gives them feedback on their performance. Ask about the performance appraisal system. How does it work? Who's involved? Do you set performance goals with your boss? Is it tied to a career development plan? Are rewards attached to performance? What's the general feeling among employees about the performance appraisal system? When and how will you be initially evaluated? Is there a probationary period? How does it work?

Question: How stressful is this job?

Try to get some idea of the level of stress involved in this job. Is this a job or a life? Are you, for example, expected to work 60 and 80 hour weeks? On a scale of 1 to 10, how stressful is this job? How do most employees handle stress? How does the company handle deadlines? Is there lots of crisis management?

> **Question:** Ideally, what type of person would do well in this position?

This question gets at the heart of expected qualifications and behavioral characteristics for the position. It lets the interviewer know that you would like to become their next star employee. Try to get the interviewer to go beyond technical qualifications, education, and training and focus more on personality, interpersonal characteristics, work style, communication skills, and specific behaviors that seem to be most conducive for performing well in this position. Ask about an example of a star performer—what type of person is this in their organization? What do they do that's different from other employees?

QUESTIONS ABOUT THE COMPANY

Questions about the company should focus on the general health of the organization and opportunities available for career growth.

> **Question:** Why did you join this organization and stay this long?

While ostensibly a motivational question, it may reveal some important aspects of the organization you may not be aware of at this point. The individual may talk about the nature of the work, the career opportunities, the people he works with, the growing nature of the business, stock options, and the personal rewards. Listen carefully for clues—both positive and negative. If, for example, he says nothing about the joy of working here or the wonderful people he interacts with, this may be a sign that the work and people are less than satisfying. Follow-up with a few additional probing questions, like "Is this the best job you've ever had?" or "Have you made lots of friends here at work?"

> **Question:** What are your long-range plans at this company?

This question will indicate whether or not the company has in place a career development plan for its employees. The answer to this question also will tell you something about vision within the organization. Do employees see a long-term future here or are they just working day by day?

> **Question:** What do you like or dislike about this company?

This is the organizational equivalent of the strengths/weaknesses question asked of interviewees. Chances are the individual will focus on the "likes" which can be very telling, especially in what is not said about the company.

> **Question:** If you had to do it over again, would you join this firm?

This is another question that gets at the positives and negatives of working for the company. You might follow-up with this related question: "If there is any one thing you would change about this company, what would it be?"

> **Question:** What do you see as some of the company's major challenges over the next five years?

This question should yield some very useful information about the company that would help you better focus your answers to the interviewer's question. It should reveal some of the major problems that need to be resolved, problems that you will probably be involved in solving. Consider following up with this question: "How do you see this position in relation to these challenges." The answer will probably reveal exactly what the employer is looking for in a candidate—solve specific problems or take on new challenges that contribute to the growth of the organization.

> **Question:** How would you evaluate the financial future of this company?

Unless you are a turnaround manager who thrives on distressed situations, chances are you want to work for a financially stable and growing organization. If you join an organization that is contracting and cutting back, you may be entering a situation characterized by low morale and crisis management. These are not fun places to work nor to build a career.

> **Question:** Who are your major competitors?

The answers to this question will give you some idea as to who is important to the company. It also may open up a new line of questioning, especially if you have some inside knowledge of the competitors that would be of interest to the interviewer. This is a good time to demonstrate your knowledge and experience.

> **Question:** Do you usually promote from within or hire from outside?

This is another question that provides some indication of the internal personnel practices and opportunities for advancement. The response will probably indicate that some positions are filled from the outside while most others are filled from the inside. This will give you some indication about how far you can advance within the organization.

> **Question:** Do you have plans to expand in the future?

The answer to this question will indicate the company's goals for the future. Most companies want to grow. Growth presents new opportunities and rewards for employees. If this company doesn't want to grow, try to find out why.

Question: If you had to describe this company in five words, what would they be?

The answer to this question will be very revealing both in terms of what is said and not said. Hopefully, a few of the five words will emphasize a positive work environment.

Question: Assuming I do an excellent job, where do you see me in five years?

The answer to this question will give you a good idea of how far and rapidly you can expect to advance in this organization. You might follow-up with this validation question: "As for the last two people who held this position, what are they doing now?"

Question: Does the company provide in-house training?

Since keeping up-to-date with skills is so important to today's workplace, it's important to know whether or not your future employer will be contributing to your career development. It also gives an indication of the company's competitiveness. Savvy employers constantly train and retrain their employees in order to maintain a talented workforce. Make sure you are working for such an employer!

Question: Most companies have some degree of internal politics. What's it like here?

This may be a sensitive question for some interviewers, especially if the organization has a bad case of debilitating politics. Nonetheless, ask it now or suffer the consequences later. Many new employees report the worst thing about their new job is the politics. They did not anticipate the group dynamics, the back biting, the petty infighting, the power struggles. You might ask this question indirectly by saying, "I've worked in companies where the internal politics was really stressful and dysfunctional for many employees who didn't want to play the games. What's been your experience here? Would I be expected to become part of someone's group? Is this a controversial hiring decision? Do I need to be careful in whom I trust?"

> ## Question: Can you tell me something about the management system here?

Try to find out about the management style. Is it conducive to individual initiative and team building? Will you be given a great deal of autonomy or will you be closely supervised? Ask some additional questions, such as "How do supervisors see their role?" and "Who will be my immediate supervisor?"

> ## Question: Could I take a tour of the company?

At some point in the interviewing process, you should be given a tour of the facilities as well as meet other individuals that would be important to the position and who are involved in the hiring process. This usually takes place at the end of the interview and indicates some interest in you. If you don't get an invitation to tour, it doesn't necessarily mean they are not interested in you. They simply may not see this tour as important in their selection process. Ask the question, because you really would like to know where and with whom you would be working. The tour also will give you new opportunities to ask additional questions about the job and company. You'll also be able to schmooze along the way and thus get a feel for the interpersonal environment.

QUESTIONS ABOUT THE INDUSTRY

Many of these questions demonstrate your larger knowledge of what's going on in the industry and market place. Hopefully, you've done a great deal of research on both the company and the industry and are prepared to ask intelligent questions relating to both.

Question: The industry as a whole has been growing at a healthy 10% per annum during the last five years. How does your company compare to this industry average?

The answer to this question will help you put the company in a large industry perspective. If it's growing at a higher or lower rate than average, follow up with questions concerning the reasons for such growth rates.

Question: I've noticed many companies have developed an aggressive e-commerce strategy. What's happening here in terms of e-commerce?

The question will give you some indication of how the company is adapting to new markets. If it is not involved in e-commerce, you need to find out why they have not moved in this direction. If they have just begun, find out what their plans are for e-commerce. Find out how your position might relate to those initiatives. If this is an area of great interest to you, let the interviewer know about your interest and expertise in this area. Perhaps you will bring some fresh ideas and talents into this area.

Question: Many mergers and restructures have taken place during the past few years in our industry. Do you see this as a possibility here?

You don't want to take a position and then suddenly find out the company has merged and you're out of a job due to the consolidation. Ask about their plans in this area. If this is a risky business because of ongoing merger and restructuring talks, be sure to include this consideration in your salary negotiations. Perhaps you need to talk about stock options, especially if the company will soon be going public as it merges.

> **Question:** Where do you see this industry going in the next five years?

Based on your research and experience, you should know this industry well. Now it's time to get the interviewer to reveal his reading of industry trends based upon his unique position in the industry. You may learn some interesting things that you hadn't thought about, such as this company is playing a leading role in developing certain trends.

> **Question:** This product line has been very popular in Asia. Do you plan to move into the Asian market in the near future?

In addition to demonstrating your knowledge of the industry, with this question you may be opening a door for future expansion of the company's operation. If you're especially knowledgeable about the Asian market, the company may be impressed with your ideas.

QUESTIONS ABOUT THE SELECTION PROCESS

You should never leave an interview without setting the stage for feedback and follow-up. However, most interviewees get to the end of the interview, shake hands, and say good-bye. They indicate little or no interest in the position. They're not sure what comes next because they haven't asked and the interviewer hasn't revealed what he or she will be doing next. In addition, the interviewer got no indication of interest on the part of the interviewee. So the interviewee returns home and waits and waits and waits, talks to himself or herself about how well he or she did in the interview, and hopes to hear from the interviewer. Waiting is not a good job search strategy, especially after conducting a job interview. You can help this process along by asking a few questions near the end of the job interview which, in effect, become key follow-up actions.

> **Question:** How many people are you interviewing for this position?

It's okay to ask about your competition—it indicates interest in the position as well as gives you useful information. The answer to this question will indicate how much interest and competition there is in this position. An alternative question is "How many applications did you receive for this position?" If the number is high, feel good that you've made it this far! As you leave the interview, let the interviewer know you are interested in the position.

> **Question:** Do I have the type of experience and qualifications you're looking for?

Try to get some immediate feedback from the interviewer. There may be some questions about your experience and qualifications the interviewer hasn't asked you. Try to get him or her to articulate these concerns so you can deal with them at this time.

> **Question:** Who makes the final hiring decision?

You may discover the final hiring decision takes place two levels above the interviewer. As such, it may involve a few weeks of decision-making. This also will tell you how far up the decision-making ladder you have climbed so far. Maybe you'll have to come back for the fourth or fifth interview in order to reach the top decision-makers.

> **Question:** As I've indicated, I'm very interested in this position. It's really a perfect fit for me. If you don't mind, I'd like to get some feedback on my candidacy. How well did things go today? Is there anything I need to do or say that would convince you to offer me the position? I think we'll work very well together.

This is a very forward way to put in a final pitch for the position. Obviously, this individual is very interested in the position and lets the interviewer know in no uncertain terms. Unlike most other candidates, this one knows something about employers that many interviewees forget—employers want you to want to work for them. They're not looking for hungry employees but ones that really feel they'll love working for them. This combination statement/question says it all!

> **Question:** I've really enjoyed meeting you. I'm very interested in the position. What is the next step?

This is a very nice closing that when said with enthusiasm emphasizes that the individual wants the position. The response should be to outline the remaining selection procedures. This person should have an idea when this process comes to a close and when they might be asked back for another interview and/or job offer.

> **Question:** When do you expect to make a final decision?

This question puts you on a calendar. Most interviewers will have some idea of when they plan to reach a decision. If the person responds by saying, "Within the next five days," go to the next question.

Question: If I don't hear from you within the next five days, would it be okay for me to call you?

This questions opens the door to making a follow-up phone call. Most interviewers will give you permission to call. Be sure to call at the expected time. If they haven't made a decision, let them know you are still interested and ask if it's okay that you call back in a couple of days. Keep calling until you get a definitive answer.

QUESTIONS ABOUT COMPENSATION

Most questions concerning compensation should be asked at the very last interview, *after* you have been offered the job. You should never raise such questions. Let the interviewer be the first to ask about salary and benefits. We examine these questions in the next chapter.

10

Negotiating the Offer

The salary question can arise anytime during a job interview. It can even arise during the initial application process or during a telephone screening interview when you are asked for your salary history or your salary requirements. When you are asked at this initial stage, the employer usually is trying to screen candidates in or out from further consideration based on financial criteria.

Premature Salary Discussions

If and when the salary question arises, your best strategy is to postpone the discussion until the very last interview—when you are offered the job. The reason for doing so is simple: you need to know the value of the position, as well as communicate your value to the employer, *before* you discuss compensation. If you talk about money before you finish this valuation process, you may prematurely undersell yourself or eliminate yourself from further consideration. If, for example, the interviewer asks you, "What are your salary requirements?" the best response is to say, "If you don't mind, I would rather discuss that issue later, after we've had a chance to discuss the requirements for this job and my qualifications." Alternatively, you can turn the question around by saying, "What do you normally pay someone with my qualifications?" This question may elicit a specific figure or salary range. Even if the figure is low, you will eventually need to discuss other compensation issues such as signing bonuses, stock options, insurance, incentivized pay, and perks that can add considerably to the total compensation package. But this can't realistically be done until after an offer is made. For now, you're better off delaying a definitive response to the salary question.

A good rule to follow is this: never discuss salary until you have been offered a job. The tendency is for employers to raise the salary question before offering the job because they see salary as a determinant in offering a position. Again, resist this temptation by raising this question: "Since we are discussing salary, am I to assume you are offering me the position?" If the answer is "yes," then proceed to negotiate salary.

> *A good rule to follow is this: never discuss salary until you have been offered a job.*

PREPARATION

Many candidates do well in the job interview but falter when it comes to talking about money. Anxious to get a job offer, some candidates accept the first figure an employer offers. As a result, they may undervalue themselves. Since annual salary increments often tend to be based on a percentage of one's gross salary figure, over time many people may be short-changing themselves by thousands of dollars because they failed to properly negotiate their initial salary.

Part of the reluctance to talk about money is cultural—many people were taught not to talk about salaries and thus they are not used to dealing with the specifics of salary and benefits. Part of the problem is the lack of preparation—they do not know what to say and do both before and during the salary negotiation session. With a little preparation, including sample dialogues to overcome any cultural reluctance to discuss money, you should be able to go into the salary negotiation session and come out with a very satisfactory compensation package.

Before talking about compensation, you need to do your homework. Like other aspects of the job search, preparation is the key to a successful salary negotiation.

The very first thing you need to do in preparation for your salary negotiation session is to **determine your market value**. After all, how can you intelligently talk about salary unless you first know what both you and the position are worth? You need some hard data so you can talk about the realities of compensation with your perspective employer. Start by seeking answers to these two questions:

- What exactly am I worth in today's job market?

- What do others in comparable positions, companies, and communities normally make?

If you are planning to make a community move, you also need to gather information on cost of living differentials.

So where are you going to get data on salary comparables? It's much easier than many people think. Numerous salary surveys are regularly conducted that yield a great deal of salary information. The major sources include the following:

1. **Government salary surveys:** Numerous federal, state, and local government agencies regularly conduct salary surveys. Check with your local library for surveys relevant to your position and industry. A good summary source for many of these government surveys is the annual directory, ***American Salaries and Wages Survey*** (Gale Research).

2. **Internet sites:** Numerous sites on the Internet provide linkages to hundreds of salary surveys. Others sell salary survey information. And still others include interactive salary calculators which primarily compare cost of living differentials between communities. Some of the most popular such sites include:

   > *http://jobsmart.org*
   > *www.abbott-langer.com*
   > *www.experienceondemand.com*
   > *www.rhii.com*
   > *www.wageweb.com*

If you are an executive making in excess of $500,000 a year, be sure to check out the Securities and Exchange Commission's site: *www.sec.gov*.

Many of the online employment sites (*www.careers.wsj.com*), as well as relocation sites, include "salary calculators" that enable you to compare how far your current salary will go in other communities that have either a higher or lower standard of living. For example, you may learn that your $60,000 salary in Peoria, Illinois will need to be at least $80,000 in San Francisco just to stay even with the local cost of living. Therefore, when negotiating a salary in San Francisco, consider your last salary to be comparable to $80,000 rather than the $60,000 you actually earned in Peoria.

3. **Professional associations:** Many professional associations conduct annual salary surveys of their members. The data is often broken down by positions, years of experience, geographic location, and salary and benefits. Contact your relevant professional association for the latest salary data on their members. This data is often accessed by employers to make sure they are offering competitive compensation. You, too, should have the advantage of this data.

4. **Publications:** Many general and specialized publications conduct annual salary surveys which, in turn, are included on the publications' Web sites. Individuals in the publishing industry, for example, turn to *Publishers Weekly's* annual salary survey for information on salary comparables. *The Wall Street Journal, Chronicle of Higher Education, Adweek, Fortune, Inc.*, and *Public Relations Journal* are just a few of many publications that publish annual salary surveys. *Compensation Review* also provides lots of useful data on salaries and benefits to keep compensation specialists current within their respective industries.

5. **Personal survey:** You also may want to conduct your own personal salary survey by asking friends, colleagues, and persons outside your company what the going salary range and benefits are for the position in question. Your personal survey may yield the most valid and useful information for your purposes. Rather than put these people on the spot by asking about their salaries and benefits, approach them by asking this indirect "research" question: "I'm conducting a salary survey to get a better idea of compensation for X position in Y industry in Z community. Would you have some idea of the going salary range and benefits for this position or would you know someone who might have such informa-

tion?" You may be pleasantly surprised how quickly you'll get fairly accurate compensation data from this survey question.

Functions, companies, industries, and geography also help to define your market value in more direct ways. A particular position, Human Resource Manager for example, will have a different market value relative to how it is perceived in each of these categories. Ask yourself the following questions:

- How is the function viewed (prestige) in each category?
- What is the size and strength of the organization?
- How does the organization rate its compensation program? (In developing a total, integrated program a Compensation Manager may place salary ranges for particular positions within the framework of the categories discussed here, then define them as in the top third or quadrant, middle third or quadrant, or upper third or quadrant of the average.)
- Is the industry in a state of growth, stasis, or decline?
- What is the cost of living in the area? (There are many good surveys here, including those published by local and national representatives of the Chamber of Commerce.)

If the Human Resource Manager position was perceived as critical to the organization, in a function recognized for its contributions, and at a pivotal moment in the organization's history, then its market value would be at a premium. Put the same position in an area with a high cost of living, such as California or Massachusetts, and the market value increases accordingly. The inverse is also true, however. If the Human Resources Manager position was perceived as a perfunctory one, necessary to fend off lawsuits but an obstacle along the path to profitability—especially in a struggling organization—then the market value would be correspondingly low. Place the position in Mississippi or Oklahoma and the value would decrease even further.

If you are unable to get the quality of compensation information you require or if you would like to test your data in a more immediate application, turn to the Internet and your network. There is an abundance of information available in both places, and you can direct it toward your specific interests. For example, a recent client was expecting an offer for a position of Knowledge Specialist. Since this was a new position in the emerging information consulting industry, it had yet to appear in any of the published surveys. The client, a Ph.D. from one of the top ten schools in the nation, had an excellent research and product development background, but was not sure if he could carry his current salary in making such a career change. He went back to his network to ask a few individuals what they thought the position should be worth. Not only did he receive some excellent input directly, but one individual referred him to a Knowledge Specialist who had conducted a survey of colleagues across the Internet. Armed with this point of reference, the client was able to negotiate a package that not only met his current salary level but included a future bonus package as well.

STRATEGY

The last major step before the negotiating process is to develop a strategy. Make sure whatever approach you take is one that you will be comfortable with and one that is compatible with your personal style. Re-examine your overall goals for both your career and the negotiation process to make certain all priorities are in sync. If you are going to use the position as a bridge to change functions, for example, you will probably want to structure your negotiations in such a way that skills and responsibilities you feel are essential to the next step are brought to the fore. You may accomplish this in a variety of ways: by expanding or emphasizing particular areas of the job description, by constructing bonuses or incentives tied to these areas, by laying the ground work for future movement, or by linking frequent performance reviews and salary actions to critical skills and responsibilities.

Remember you are not alone in the process. There are the proverbial two sides to every story, and you need to recognize the employer's needs as well as your own. Be prepared for the obligatory give and take. Try to anticipate an employer's questions and concerns. Prepare responses; run through a number of hypothetical situations, so you may be as confident and comfortable as possible. It is often a good idea to practice saying your responses aloud. Certainly, the last thing you would want to happen is to have some kind of breakdown between what you are thinking and what you want to say; you neither want to be misunderstood nor misrepresented. What you will be engaged in is a dialogue. The more prepared you are, the more fluid and adaptable you will be as the dialogue unfolds.

DIALOGUE

Timing is critical. Both parties will want to choose the optimum time to negotiate. You will, of course, want to negotiate when you have the most momentum: when the future employer is more desirous of purchasing your services. On the other hand, the potential employer will want to negotiate when you are in the weakest position and a variety of potential employees are still in the running for the position. That is why you want to negotiate at **the moment the position is offered,** while the employer wants to address salary issues at the beginning of the first interview (or before, as in a request in an advertisement to state salary requirements or salary history).

Consider the following diagram:

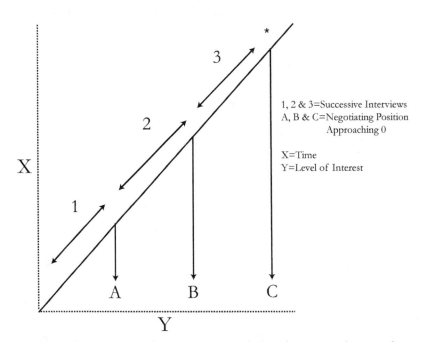

The above graph depicts the correlation between the number of interviews, level of interest, and strength of negotiating position; clearly, the greater the number of interviews, the more intense the interest and the more enhanced the negotiating position. (See the ascending line marked by 1, 2, and 3.) Conversely, if the interviewer decides there is not a match, the company's interest in you for the position and your possibility of negotiating plummets to zero. (See A and B.) The apex of the graph, or the point of greatest interest (indicated by the *), occurs where an offer is formally tendered. This, of course, is where you should negotiate. For if you fail to negotiate at this point—especially if you accept the offer—your negotiating position is essentially nil. (See C.)

In the early stages of the first interview, the interviewer has little or no commitment to you and holds the dominant position. Even during the initial screening interview, you can expect a series of questions which will try to pinpoint your compensation expectations in order to determine if you fit into the company salary structure. Your most effective strategy at this point revolves around deferring all salary discussions until a position has been tendered, while assuring the interviewer that compensation would not be a problem; moreover, you would like to demonstrate what you can do for the organization; and you would like to explore the possibilities of a match in greater detail.

When you are asked such questions, make certain your responses are consistent in terms of tone, level of sophistication, and point of reference with your personality and overall delivery. Some possible questions you may encounter, as well as potential responses, would include the following:

Question: **What kind of salary are you looking for? How much do you want to make? What income do you expect?**

Answer: Well, Mr. Andrews, at this point, I'm very flexible. If we determine there's a good fit here, I'm sure we'll be able to work out a very reasonable agreement. I'd appreciate it if we could just postpone those discussions for now; and once we agree on a fit, I'm sure we'll be able to work out the rest. Can you tell me more about the position? What are you looking for in the ideal candidate?

Question: **What did you make in your last (present) position?**

Answer: I'm not at liberty to discuss that. I've made an agreement not to discuss salary, benefits, or any internal policies of that position. (Use this, of course, only if you

have made such an agreement.) I'm sure you can respect my loyalty in that regard. But anyway, I'm flexible, and I'm sure we can work something out after we
determine if there is a good fit here. Can you tell me
what a typical day would be like?

Question: **You'll need to give me some idea what you expect,
so we can see if we're in the ballpark here. What's
the minimum you would accept?**

Answer: Well, Mr. Andrews, I'm trying to remain very open
minded and flexible on that issue, but I can see how
important it is to you to determine a ballpark figure.
(Pause) Tell you what. You have a better idea of the
overall value this position has for the company than I
do, and I'm sure there's a range established that we'll
both have to live with. If you would give me some idea
of what that range is, I'll be glad to tell you if I'm interested in discussing this position any further.

Question: **(Whatever they say...)**

Answer: Certainly I'm interested in continuing discussions on that
basis. Tell me more about the position.

Question: **What would it take to bring you on board?**

Answer: Is that an offer?

Question: **Yes.**

Answer: Well, what range did you have in mind?

The overall success of your negotiations is also dependent upon
creating the optimum environment. You need to be confident and articulate yet relaxed. Put the interviewer at ease. Remember, the negotiating arena knows few experts, and the interviewer may be a novice in
the field. The greater the level of comfort you can establish here, the
greater the possibility of reward later.

Recognize the interviewer, not only in terms of success but in relation to position and function. Grant interviewers, as Henry James would

of writers, their *doneé*. Know what is their "given." For example, the range of reference points—and, of course, questions and approaches—may differ wildly depending upon the interviewer's function and position in the company. As a rule of thumb, the higher the position and the closer to your function, the greater the possibility of you achieving your negotiation objectives, because the interviewer will have a better understanding of what you bring to the table as well as a greater control over budgetary impact.

In the first interview scenario discussed above, the dynamics would probably be quite different if the questions were posed by a Human Resources Manager or a Sales Manager. In the former instance, the HR Manager is probably referring to a barometer to determine if you could fit into the appropriate category for position, years of experience, and salary. If you apparently did not fit, you would be screened out of the process. Further, unless you were applying for a Human Resources position, you could probably assume that the interviewer was not an expert in your field and your strongest arguments for the position would be greatly diminished. On the other hand, if the interviewer were the hiring manager in a specific function, you might anticipate greater flexibility in salary issues and a clearer understanding of what you bring to the table. As a result, you could marshal your most compelling arguments (and to a more sympathetic ear) to advance to the next round of interviews, to defer further discussion of compensation, and to enhance your negotiating position.

WIN-WIN STRATEGIES

Regardless of the interviewer's position, however, you should always try to create a win-win atmosphere. Approach negotiations as a collaborative effort. Don't forget you are negotiating with an individual(s) with whom you will be working—often with the person who will be your direct manager. It is not the time to play hardball, but it is the time to lay the foundation for open communication and long-term growth. You have the opportunity to set yourself up for failure by being confrontational or for success by working as a team and creating the type of harmony the Japanese refer to as *wa*.

On a practical level, eschew the use of antithetical personal pronouns and other dichotomies that emphasize the differences between both parties. Try to bridge gaps and foster a sense of mutual purpose.

Client Feedback

"I am very proud to say that by applying the get tough attitude you inspired in me, even when the going was unbearable, I was offered, and accepted, a position that pays more than the upper end of the average pay scale for my profession. By keeping the $1,000 per minute tactics in mind during all phases of salary negotiations, even under extreme pressure, I was able to increase my initial salary by $6,000 within two weeks with the same company."

—S.B.

Use "we," for example, rather than the "I/you" split that emphasizes your positions on opposite sides of the negotiating table. You will find this much more beneficial in the long term. For example, let's assume that the negotiation dialogue had followed all the positive, collaborative criteria we have discussed so far, yet you still had come to an impasse on salary and remained ten thousand dollars apart. At this point you certainly do not want the negotiations to break down. Presenting a viable option or compromise would probably allow the process to continue, but it would be up to you to take the next step. You might suggest, "What if *we* looked at some other options," and direct the negotiations to other compensation areas, such as incentives, bonuses, or perquisites. (Refer to the Negotiation Checklist at the end of this chapter for an overview of compensation possibilities.). Or if there appears to be no income options, examine issues of vacation or reviews. A good compromise position is to propose a six month and a twelve month performance review and salary action in place of the typical annual one. But again, make certain to emphasize mutual benefit and commitment: "What if *we* look at…"

If you review our discussion so far, you will note that there have been a great number of references to the personalities involved. It is not an accident. Negotiations occur in real time and in real space, not in some abstract vacuum. For each individual—you and the company representative(s)—brings to the process particular emotional vested interests that could have a profound effect upon the overall negotiations.

Consequently, you must be totally aware of where your emotional issues lay and strive to identify those of the interviewer.

Try to put yourself in the interviewer's position. Are there any identifiable elements of stress? Is the company struggling under any immediate production or delivery timetables that would pressure the interviewer to bring the process to a quick resolution? Has a previous candidate turned down the offer or proven to be an unfortunate choice once on the job? If so, the interviewer may be placed in a must close situation or, at least, in a position where the competitive edge may fall to you.

Once you have identified the interviewer's emotional issues, integrate them into the negotiation process as you earlier incorporated your knowledge of the company's problems into your argument that you were the perfect fit for the position. Do not dwell on them, making them appear as significant obstacles; rather, use them as a platform to re-emphasize your value to the organization and to improve your bargaining stance. For example, if you recognize time to be a critical element for the interviewer ("we need someone to start next week") and a negotiable one for you, try to meet the company's deadlines. It will take the pressure off the interviewer, demonstrate your ability to work with others, and increase your chances of negotiating something else.

Do not forget, however, that you too have emotional issues that could affect the dynamics of the process. Hopefully, you have identified these far in advance of actual negotiations. At any rate, review your priorities and preparation. Make sure all elements are part of a cohesive, comprehensive strategy. Recognize how you would react if certain sensitive issues were brought up. Prepare responses (while remaining flexible), and practice articulating them to avoid stumbling and compromising your position.

For example, health insurance may be a pressing issue with you. If there are family or personal medical situations that make this benefit imperative to you, it is likely that your response here would be an emotional one. Try not to let your feelings throw the negotiation process out of balance. The more time you spend on this subject—particularly if you make it a pivotal element during negotiations—the less likely you are to achieve other compensation goals. Objectify the process; do not confound emotional value with market value. Health benefits tend to be standard throughout an organization—you may negotiate COBRA payments or enrollment periods. If you frequently return to this issue, you may gain a point (that was a given anyway) only to concede others later.

FOCUS ON THE BIG PICTURE

You should always, as the example above illustrates, keep in mind the big picture—the entire compensation package. It is easy to get obsessed with a part and lose track of the whole. The history of real estate transactions is littered with cases of individuals who lost an opportunity to negotiate thousands of dollars off the price of a home for the privilege of retaining the rights to an $800 chandelier. Do not fall into the same trap.

Examine the compensation package in *toto*. (Refer to the Negotiation Checklist at the end of this section for a good overview.) Establish a general monetary and critical value for the whole as well as each part; specifically, isolate all the components and determine the value of each—not only on the open market but to you personally. For example, if a company has a 100% tuition reimbursement policy, its market value could be worth thousands of dollars per year depending on the college or university, number and level of classes. If you intended to pursue your formal education, this would be an exciting benefit whose value to you would be at least equal to that of the market and perhaps greater if it proved to be both an incentive and a springboard to career growth. On the other hand, if you chose not to take any classes, its value to you would be zero regardless of what it would bear on the market. In either case, the dynamics of the process would be affected and you would have to make certain once again your strategy and priorities were in sync with your overall approach.

> *You must choose your battles very carefully. Not every item will be negotiated. Keep the items you perceive as critical in the foreground; place the rest in the background or drop them altogether.*

A central element in maintaining a larger perspective is understanding the ebb and flow of the negotiation process itself. Remember, this is not a union negotiation session where you would be negotiating line item by line item. You must choose your battles very carefully. Not every item will be negotiated. Keep the items you perceive as critical in the foreground; place the rest in the background or drop them altogether.

Try to get the interviewer to name the first figure. Salespersons, rug dealers, negotiators, all would agree: "The first to speak is the first to lose."

One of the most important elements of choosing your battles is knowing which ones may even be fought. The first step here is to refer back to the entire compensation package to determine which items have the potential to be negotiated. Most benefits are standardized and offered to all equally; these can not be negotiated. You will want to keep in mind precisely what they are, however, so you can plan a negotiating strategy. On the other hand, many of the items in a compensation package may be negotiated. As a rule of thumb, most of the entries under the following headings in the Negotiation Checklist may be negotiable: Basic Compensation Issues, Vacation and Time Issues, Perquisites, Relocation Expenses, Home Office Options, and (for senior executives) Severance Packages. Again, keep in mind that you will not be negotiating each line item but only those that fit your strategy and the unfolding of your personal negotiations.

Be very careful with language; it is often as important how you say something as it is what you say. Our earlier comments on creating the optimum atmosphere and recognizing emotional issues are critical here. You will want to be sensitive to tone as well as to the denotation (definition) and connotation (secondary meaning, association, implication) of words. For example, the word "contract" has very strong connotations and conjures up visions of liability, control, and restraint. Yet you could often acquire the benefits of a written agreement without ever threatening the progress of the negotiations simply by avoiding the term "contract." Rather, after you have completed the negotiations and before you have accepted the position, you might say, "Everything sounds great. If you don't mind, fax me a copy of what we agreed upon. I'll look it over and we can finalize things then." This tact would appear personable and professional without seeming litigious and would essentially accomplish the same result as a "contract."

Once the negotiations have started, begin with a discussion of base salary. Try to get the interviewer to name the first figure. This will not only give you a specific point of reference, but it will also give you the stronger position with the most negotiating options. The interviewer has, in effect, been bound on one side and has limited flexibility. You, conversely, still have all options available to you. Salespersons, rug dealers, negotiators, all would agree: "The first to speak is the first to lose."

When the initial figure is named, repeat it to make sure there is absolutely no confusion about this number. (See Sample Negotiation Dialogue on pages 175–180.) Once agreement is acknowledged, respond with silence. At this juncture, silence may be your strongest negotiating tool. Most individuals are uncomfortable with the pause and will want to fill the space, particularly if the pause is extended. You would want to use thirty seconds as a benchmark. (If you have a difficult time remaining quiet for this time, try counting to thirty slowly in your head—one thousand and one . . . one thousand and two...) If the interviewer breaks the silence, it is frequently to increase the offer. Though the process can not go on indefinitely, you may want to repeat it once more to see if you can increase the offer again.

Soon, however, you must respond with a number. To maintain your flexibility, work with a range when you have to respond with a number. If the interviewer, for example, has offered you $48,000, your counter may be something "approaching $60,000." At this point the interviewer would probably focus on $60,000, yet the number could really represent a vast range. You may choose instead to imply a range or state a specific range: the "mid fifties," for example, or "$54,000 to $58,000." In each of the above cases, you have avoided a level of specificity that would tie you to a specific number, and you have retained maximum flexibility.

Remember, that whatever your market value, you still must fit within the employer's salary structure. These two issues, market value and salary structure, should be integrated in order for there to be an ideal fit. Naturally, you would want the employer's range to meet or exceed the upper limit of your market value, though it is also possible that the range may be low to middle—or even below—market value. This is a point at which you must reflect once again upon the match—goals, environment, growth possibilities, compensation package—to reassure yourself of the fit.

CONSIDER OPTIONS

If you believe the offer is not in an acceptable range and the employer's salary structure is out of sync with your market value, you will want to explore other options with the employer. You may, for instance, look at the job title and how it corresponds to the pay grade. It may be possible to upgrade the job title—and, hence, the compensation—without upsetting the employer's salary structure; certainly a winning situation for both of you. Similarly, you may want to explore expanding the range of authority and responsibility for the position as a manner of enhancing compensation while maintaining the balance inherent in a salary structure.

You will want to get the best compensation package possible that is both fair and equitable. It is, of course, the purpose of the negotiations. However, you must be careful throughout the process to keep the negotiations positive and upbeat. If the potential employer feels cornered, you may get the money you demanded, but it may be difficult to recreate the feeling of cooperation necessary to be at peak effectiveness on the job. In the worst possible scenario you could even be set up for failure by being given a set of performance goals that would be impossible to achieve. Likewise, and here a recognition of the employer's salary structure is critical, you would not want your salary to become an albatross, crippling your chances of growth, movement, and longevity in the organization. If you can not justify your compensation, in short, you should not be paid it. (The implication here is you should always be able to verify your worth to an organization.) Consider the following scenario:

> An Operations Manager has held the same position in a large corporation for the past ten years. The corporation is going through a period of streamlining budgets and downsizing staff. Though the Vice President (Operations Manager's boss) would very much like to keep the Operations Manager, the contingencies of the budget argue against it. In an attempt to save the position the Vice President calls the Operations Manager in and asks bluntly for a justification of salary. "John, you know the

kind of budget crunch we're under. I'm getting pressure from above to reduce salaries, and I have been looking yours over. You are making 75% more than when you were first promoted. I want to keep you on—I believe we work well together—but I need something concrete to take to the President. Prove to me you are 75% better than when you started, and I'll have a solid argument for the budget."

Seldom would you see a situation so baldly stated, yet it crystallizes a critical point. If, in fact, the Operations Manager could not argue the point cogently and forcefully, there would be essentially no option but outplacement or executive clemency. If you place yourself in a position of relying on corporate goodwill, you would be wise to avoid anyone who offers to sell you a piece of the Brooklyn Bridge. Once salary issues are decided or tabled, begin to explore the possibilities of performance bonuses and/or incentives. (In certain, very particular cases, this would also include equity issues such as stock, percentages of the company, ownership, and so on.) Inherent in each of these situations is a verification of your compensation; you will not receive any additional monies unless you have achieved your goals which, in turn, are linked to corporate objectives.

When you are looking at bonuses and incentives, make sure you tie them to items you directly affect. If, for example, you are hired as a Materials Manager and one of your responsibilities is inventory, try to connect incentives to bottom line issues such as inventory reduction. Perhaps, you would be hired to institute a JIT system by January 1. Should you expect a bonus if you accomplished this goal? No, because that is what you were hired to do. However, if the company gained some competitive advantage by converting to the new system earlier, you would want to link that possibility to a bonus. So, if you hit your objective by December 1, you would like a bonus; by November 1, a larger one; by October 1, something very significant.

> *When you are looking at bonuses and incentives, make sure you tie them to items you directly affect.*

"Something very significant" sounds quite exciting, but you would, of course, want to be much more specific. Determining how and when the bonus will be paid, how it will be set up, and how it will be measured are crucial aspects of the negotiation process. In terms of payment, most individuals would prefer their remuneration to be based on percentages rather than fixed amounts, because there would be a much greater chance of higher income. Conversely, most companies are hesitant to pay from percentages unless there is a higher than normal risk or unless the organization can also expect a significant payoff. In our Materials Management example, you would want to try to get an inventory reduction incentive based on percentages, though you should be aware this would be a very difficult sell. Your argument for percentages would be most apt to be received if: (1) the company were experiencing cash flow problems due to excess of out-of-date inventory; (2) the company had a history of incentivizing pay; and/or (3) you made an excellent case for your proposal, citing specific issues, measurements, and strategies—particularly in terms of the benefits to the company. Even if the company were reluctant to offer a percentage based incentive, it would seem an ideal time—as the JIT scenario above—to negotiate a fixed amount bonus.

Regardless of how an incentive is paid, you would want both the pay periods and measurements to occur as frequently as possible. The more opportunities you have to reach your incentives, the more opportunities you will have to increase your income. Consider the following illustration:

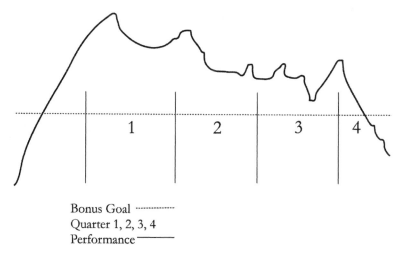

Bonus Goal ············
Quarter 1, 2, 3, 4
Performance ———

If you were approaching bonuses based on annualized performance (this is, of course, a strong tendency in the workplace), you would not receive a bonus for the year due to an unfortunate turn of events in the final quarter. On the other hand, if you had tied the bonuses to quarterly performance, you could anticipate payouts for the first, second, and third quarters. Further, if you have linked bonuses to even shorter time frames, months for instance, you could increase the possibility of payouts even more often.

If you have agreed in principle to what the incentives are linked to and how the compensation is to be based, you should proceed to the next level of detail—measurements. For example, if you were to be paid a sales commission, would it be based on the number of sales? New sales? Total revenues? Profit? New markets? Specific products? The possibilities are nearly infinite. If the discussion becomes more complicated than you originally anticipated, it is not a problem. You must be certain that both you and the potential employer are in full agreement on each point. The extra time and care spent here will help avoid any confusion, misunderstandings, or bad feelings in the future. Remember, you are also building a long term business partnership with the potential employer. Always keep your focus positive and your attitude professional.

RECAP, EVALUATE, AND QUERY

Be sure to recap at this juncture to make certain you have covered all your priorities. Review the agreement in its entirety to make sure both parties understand all aspects of the discussion. You may want to do this mentally if you believe everything is perfectly clear, verbally if you want to double check any item or get additional buy-in on particular points (not a bad idea).

Though you need to be prepared to agree in principle to the offer, it is not yet time to make a final commitment. Now that you are clear on every point, it is time to evaluate the offer. Ask yourself the following questions:

- Are your compensation objectives met?

- Are there opportunities to advance your income?

- Are your career goals achieved or achievable?

- Are you able to begin on a positive footing?
- Have you room to grow and develop?
- Have you a platform for free and open communication?
- Have you set up a time to outline your goals and performance issues?

If there are any unanswered questions, this is the appropriate time to pursue answers. If all your evaluation concerns have been addressed, it is time to proceed. However, try to be sensitive to any indications of anxiety on the part of the potential employer. It sometimes happens that there is a sense of "buyer's remorse." Don't let this happen; resell yourself. In fact, this is a critical aspect of the negotiations and should be used throughout, especially when you appear to have reached an impasse. There should never be any doubt as to what you could do for the employer.

Once there is agreement on all aspects of the offer, you need to decide whether or not to ask for the offer in writing. In general, you will want the offer in writing if:

> ### Case In Point
>
> *"Tom obtained a referral to a company executive in a small traffic signal manufacturing company. The president was conservative, set in his ways and did not want to pay much money—but he did need a controller. Tom established his price, refused to budge, walked out of negotiations twice, but is now controller and CFO of the organization."*

- you have negotiated anything out of the normal realm
- you are relocating
- you have negotiated a particularly complex agreement

There is seldom any difficulty in obtaining a positive response to this request since most employers are eager to wrap things up at this point. It is, after all, a serious business agreement, and few individuals would proceed in a business relationship without some sort of documentation.

Do not, however, accept the offer at this time. Ask for at least 24 hours to respond; this will give you plenty of time to analyze the offer and reflect on the possibilities. If you have other opportunities evolving, you may want to ask for more time, so you will have the potential to bring other offers simultaneously to the fore. In fact, the time issue is probably the last item you will negotiate.

Perhaps the most difficult element of negotiating now becomes critical. Implied throughout the process was your willingness to walk away from the deal. Up to this point in the discussion, we have been assuming a tentative agreement had been reached. However, it is also possible that the offer as stands may be unacceptable. You must be prepared, in either case, to say "no" to the offer. Keep in mind tact, diplomacy, and professionalism; you never want to burn any bridges. If you are not willing to take this step, you can never really negotiate, because you have not empowered yourself to embrace the full range of decision making responsibility.

Evaluate the offer at home or in your office. Once removed from the emotion of the negotiations you can analyze the offer more objectively. You need to be as clear as possible about the decision. Discuss it with your family; if all members are not willing to go forward, you can assume problems will surface at a later date. For example, relocation, travel, and time expectations are often minimized in the excitement of the offer. However, once you are settled in the new position, novelty gives way to reality. The strain on the family will begin to surface in many stressful ways unless all are committed to the move. Occasionally, individuals have found themselves six months after accepting an offer facing an ultimatum: job or family.

One final caution should be added. If you are either between positions or terribly unhappy with your current one, you can expect the emotion of the moment to be great. As we discussed earlier, you need to identify where your particular emotional issues lay. If this is one, don't let your heart rule your head; control the decision making process. Do not leap at any unacceptable offer simply to avoid an unpleasant situation. Ask yourself one final time the same evaluative questions we presented earlier. A "yes" response to all of the questions is a clear indication you should accept the offer. If you would have to give negative responses to a few, then you would have to get together with the potential employer one final time to iron out the differences. Finally, if you would answer "no" to all or most, the offer is clearly an unacceptable one and should be considered only as a short term, cash flow solution.

In the end, negotiating is an art and a process. While there are many guidelines to follow and options to explore, don't expect guarantees. If you keep in mind the big picture, the need for mutual cooperation, and the willingness to be flexible, you should be successful. And success here is critical, because it lays the foundation for career fulfillment—in both the short and long terms.

SAMPLE NEGOTIATION DIALOGUE

Assumptions: The potential employee, John, has done his research and knows the salary range for the position to be between $62,000 and $66,000. Throughout the interviewing process he has been very clear regarding the positive impact he can have on the organization. Likewise, he has built an atmosphere of confidence and professionalism with an emphasis on mutual benefit and cooperation. The decision maker, Susan, will be John's boss should he decide to accept the offer and begin working for the organization.

Susan: Well John, I believe we have an excellent match here, and I'm prepared to make you an offer. Quite frankly, I'm looking for real strong contributions from you and am willing to pay you accordingly ...How does $55,000 sound?

(Wants to close the deal; hence, she makes an offer that she believes is both fair and high, indicating her reluctance to move little, if at all, while implying a limit.)

John: $55,000?
(Wants to clarify the number. There cannot be a miscommunication at this point.)

Susan: Yes.

(Reassures and clarifies, keeping a positive focus)

John: *(Thoughtful pause, 30 seconds. Attempts to question without verbally doing so. Creates a pattern of give and take within the assumed response time framework . . . again, without speaking. Conveys thoughtfulness and professionalism as well as a concern for the amount suggested.)*

Susan: *(Breaking the silence.)* Tell you what; let's get things started on the right foot. I think I can go to $57,500. It may be pushing the envelope a bit, but I'm willing to go the extra mile for the extra value.
(Feels a bit uncomfortable with the silence. Assumes no response means the offer is unacceptable. Wants to fill the quiet space, be reassuring, and keep things moving in a positive direction.)

John: $57,500?
(Makes certain the figure is clear.)

Susan: Absolutely.
(Maintains upbeat posture. After all, she has just, in effect, given John a raise.)

John: *(Thoughtful pause. Wants to maintain the momentum without seeming aloof or patronizing. Recognizes the worth of repeating the process. This time great sensitivity is needed to be in tune with the dynamics of the situation. If Susan seems a bit put off, it would certainly not be attempted.)*

Susan: *(Breaking in.)* John, you're not saying much. What have you got on your mind? *(Thinks things may be getting drifty. Does not want to lose control of the interview. Takes initiative. Needs to clarify John's position.)*

John: It's an interesting offer, but considering the scope of the position, I was expecting something in, say, the mid $60's. I can be flexible, though. Let's see what we can work out.
(Has successfully moved the bottom line up $2,500. By employing effective pauses, has negotiated without naming a figure. John's

next number will be his first, though Susan has already cited two figures. John needs to give a point of reference. Something general will allow him optimal flexibility. Needs to communicate flexibility and cooperation. Makes it seem to be a mutual problem that is easy to solve.)

Susan: It's going to be hard to do much else. Remember, we have an excellent benefits package: a matching 401(K), vacation—you will have two weeks after the first year—and a medical plan that includes dental, vision, and prescription. *(Recognizes she is at, probably, the end of the salary she can offer. Wants to placate with something. Emphasizes all the benefits to make the offer appear more enticing. Appears to give something without doing more than presenting the givens.)*

> ## Case In Point
>
> *"I had just finished teaching a client how to do the 'silence technique' of negotiating (30 seconds of silence) when he was invited in for an interview. They offered him $90,000 (he's at the VP manufacturing level) and he said they all sat there quietly, not saying a word, for 2½ minutes! Then the interviewer said 'how about $100,000?' My client told them later that this was the first time he had ever negotiated."*

John: I agree; the benefits are comprehensive. I do have a question about them, but first I'd like to return to something you mentioned a moment ago—extra value. I am excited about the opportunity, and I've got to tell you, I think we do have a match. I can bring extra value to the table by creating a positive impact on your bottom line while enhancing your morale. Everywhere I've been I have been able to reduce costs by at least 15% while reducing turnover…and I intend to do the same for you.

(Understands the lines that are being drawn. Will want to return to the vacation issue, so alludes to a concern. Wants to settle all monetary issues first. Needs to resell himself in order for the company to feel good about his real value and the organization's potential ROI. Reinforces the mutual bond and benefits.)

Susan: We certainly believe you can.
(Reassures. The dynamics are constantly shifting in subtle ways. Follows the flow, taking a strong turn toward closure.)

John: We're both anxious to work this out. I do have a few concerns, but again, I can be flexible. What if we just split the difference.
(Reassures. Presents an option that appears to be win/win. Drives the momentum.)

Susan: Tell you what John; I can go $58,500, but that will be the limit.
(Wants to continue the movement toward closure. Recognizes the benefit of giving something back, but also knows the limits of the salary structure. Another $1,000 would be a very positive gesture and help build a strong bond of cooperation, helping to put the company in a much better light. Understands she needs to bring John into the company.)

John: Well, let's see what we can do with come incentive options that might make it possible to get a little nearer to the center.
(Moves toward the center, but would like to get the income potential closer to a mid point. Needs to present an alternative, particularly one that is performance based, thus creating a win/win solution.)

Susan: What did you have in mind?
(Doesn't want to lose the momentum or the deal. No harm in exploring options. Begins to think of precedents.)

John: Let's look at cost issues. As we discussed in our previous interview, there will be a specific operating budget under my control; is that correct?
(Gets initial buy-in. Isolates key issues and area of impact.)

Susan: Yes.
(Willing to proceed; probably feeling a little uncertain where the conversation will go. Remains anxious to work things out.)

John: What if we looked at a $500 bonus for each quarter I came in more than 2% under budget.
(Perceives this as the last opportunity to grow the potential income. Assumes the company is near its compensation limit. Needs to specify production and payment parameters. Chooses straight payment rather that percentages to give the company more certainty and a specific cap.)

Susan: Hmm. I think we might do that.
(Parameters are clear. Understands the only way additional monies are paid out is if the company profits financially. Performs some quick math; seems reasonable. Looks like a good, mutually beneficial situation.)

John: OK. One final thing. You mentioned a two week vacation after a year. Frankly, Susan, I'm accustomed to four weeks, but I appreciate your going out on a limb a bit for me on some of the monetary issues, so I'm willing to take a little less time than I've received in the past. Could we make it two weeks within the first year and three after that? It is an important issue to me.
(Returns to the one issue left hanging. Knows he needs to wrap things up. Uses previous compensation package to emphasize expectations. Does not want problems at this point. Reassures by demonstrating appreciation for all that has been done to this point while reiterating the importance of this final issue. Note: no actual money would be exchanged here.)

Susan: All right, John. So, we have a deal?

(Wants to acknowledge what is important. Can always work out some vacation scheme. Looks like a good compromise, but will go no further. Wants closure. Asks a question to get agreement.)

John: Everything sounds great Susan. If you don't mind, just write up what we agreed upon. Fax it to me, and we can wrap things up.

(Recognizes the need to put the offer in writing since there are some unusual aspects to the offer. May have to clarify exactly how the incentives will be measured, but that can be easily handled after reading over the offer. Wants to be as positive and reassuring as possible.)

Susan: Sounds good, I'll put something on paper and get it to you within two days.

(Moves toward closure in a positive fashion.)

John: I'd appreciate it. Thanks again, Susan. This entire discussion reaffirms my belief in the organization. I'm really looking forward to becoming a part of it.

(Maintains positive approach; shows appreciation; and resells the company on the match.)

Susan: We are too. Don't forget to call when you get the fax.

(Reaffirms company position and makes sure next step is clear, so the offer can be finalized.)

John: No problem.

(Follow-up is clear. Everyone is positive. The groundwork is laid for a successful relationship with the company, and the compensation goals have been met. Overall, it is a win/win situation.)

CHECKLIST OF COMPENSATION OPTIONS

Basic Compensation Issues

Item	Comments
❑ Base Salary	Automatic or only at times?
❑ Commissions	Be sure there is agreement on how they will be measured, how often they will be paid, and how they will be calculated (e.g. net or gross).
❑ Corporate Profit Sharing	Vesting schedule? Tied to organizational level?
❑ Personal Performance Bonuses/Incentives	Be sure there is agreement on how they will be measured, how often they will be paid, and how they will be calculated.
❑ Equity Position	Specify this carefully, especially time schedule and percentages.
❑ Cost of Living Adjustment	Independent of reviews? How often paid?
❑ Performance Reviews	
❑ Signing Bonus	Especially if bonuses/incentives for current company are lost.

Health Benefits

❑ Medical Insurance	See general comments below.
❑ Dental Insurance	
❑ Vision Insurance	
❑ Prescription Package	
❑ Life Insurance	
❑ Accidental Death & Disability Insurance	Can it be carried over after leaving the company?
❑ Periodic Medical Examinations	
❑ Assistance Programs (EAP's)	
❑ Pregnancy Package	

Determine how much you'll have to pay in these areas: What portion of your health insurance? What are the deductible and co-insurance provisions? What is the extent of coverage? (E.g. consider mental health issues.) What do you pay for office visits under a health maintenance organization? At what age are medical exams provided? How frequently?

Vacation and Time Issues

❑ Vacation Time	How much vacation time and how soon are you eligible?
❑ Sick Days	Accrued or automatic? What if you go over?
❑ Personal Time	Can it be accumulated from year to year
❑ Holidays	Which are set? Any floating?
❑ Flex Time	How is it defined?
❑ Compensatory Time	How is it tracked?
❑ Paternity/Maternity Leave	Generally accepted or specifically
❑ Family Leave	tracked?

Retirement-Oriented Benefits

❑ Defined-Benefit Plan	What is the vesting schedule? What
❑ 401 (K) Plan	is the limit of personal contribu-
❑ Deferred Compensation	tions? Of company contribu-
❑ Savings Plans	tions?
❑ Stock-Purchase Plans	
❑ Stock Bonus	Tied to income? Longevity? Posi-
❑ Stock Options	tion?
❑ Ownership/Equity	Percentages? Graduated over time? Personal/Company contributions? Buy-out? Limit? Options?

Education

❑ Professional Continuing Education	Percent or total paid? How long?
❑ Tuition Reimbursement For Yourself or Children	

Military

- ❏ Compensatory Pay During Active Duty
- ❏ National Guard

Problem getting time off?

Perquisites

- ❏ Cellular Phone

  Minutes or total bill? You negotiate or company?

- ❏ Company Car or Vehicle/ Mileage Allowance

  How much? Insurance? Personal use?

- ❏ Expense Accounts

  Limits?

- ❏ Liberalization of Business-Related Expenses

- ❏ Child Care

  In-house?

- ❏ Cafeteria Privileges

  Family or guests included?

- ❏ Executive Dining Room Privileges

  Family included?

- ❏ First-Class Hotels

  Who arranges?

- ❏ First-Class Air Travel

  Who arranges?

- ❏ Personal Use of Frequent-Flier Awards

- ❏ Convention Participation: Professionally Related

  Limited by time or number?

- ❏ Parking

- ❏ Paid Travel for Spouse

- ❏ Professional-Association Memberships

  Problem getting time off?

- ❏ Athletic Club Memberships

- ❏ Social Club Memberships

- ❏ Use of Company-Owned Facilities

  Does it extend to family?

- ❏ Executive Office

  What are the parameters of staff support?
  Of technical and material support?

- ❏ Lap-Top Computers
- ❏ Private Secretary
- ❏ Portable Fax
- ❏ Employee Discounts

Relocation Expenses

❑ Direct Moving Expenses — Total or lump sum? Choose movers?

❑ Moving Costs for Unusual Property — Works of art, pianos, antique furniture, etc.

❑ Trips to Find Suitable Housing — Expenses for self and spouse?

❑ Loss on Sale of Present Home or Lease Termination — How long will company be active? Will company purchase the house?

❑ Company Handling Sale of Present Home

❑ Housing-Cost Differential Between Cities — Use relocation guide, cost of living indexes.

❑ Mortgage-Rate Differential — Try for three years, enough time to get into the economic cycle of the community.

❑ Mortgage Fees and Closing Costs — Total or percent? Your choice of vendor?

❑ Temporary Dual Housing — How long will the company pay one or both residences?

❑ Trips Home During Dual Residency — Determine frequency and limit.

❑ Real Estate Fees

❑ Utilities Hookup

❑ Drapes/Carpets

❑ Appliance Installation

❑ Auto/Pet Shipping

❑ Signing Bonus for Incidental Expenses

❑ Additional Meals Expense Account

❑ Bridge Loan While Owning Two Homes

❑ Outplacement Assistance for Spouse — Who chooses?

Home Office Options

❏ Personal Computer

❏ Internet access

❏ Copier

❏ Printer

❏ Financial Planning Assistance

❏ Separate Phone Line

❏ Separate Fax Line

❏ CPA/Tax Assistance

❏ Incidental/Support Office Functions

❏ Office Supplies

In each instance in Home Office Options determine whether they furnish or you will bill back? Home as well as office?

Severance Packages (Parachutes)

❏ Base Salary

At the executive level six months to one year is generally appropriate. On rare occasions it could extend to a multi-year payout and/or be tied to retirement. At other levels one or two weeks pay for every year with the organization is common. In all cases consider the tax implications of lump sum verses extended pay outs.

❏ Bonuses/incentives

Ideally projected for the entire year; otherwise attempt to have them prorated.

❏ Non-Compete Clause

Negotiate time as well as compensation.

Analyze market value.

❏ Stock/Equity

Need to be sold? How soon? At what price and how is price derived?

❏ Outplacement

Preferably of your choosing. How long?

❏ Voicemail access

For a negotiated amount of time.

❑ Statement (letter) of explanation of why you left — Agreed upon by all parties.

❑ Vacation reimbursement — Who will handle? From potential employer?

❑ Health benefits — Paid, at least, over the same time period as base salary.

❑ 401(K) contributions — To continue as long as possible.

Negotiation DO's and DON'Ts

DO's

1. Develop the proper frame of mind.
2. Integrate career and negotiation goals.
3. Know your market value.
4. Develop a negotiating strategy.
5. Recognize the employer's position as well as your own.
6. Be prepared to be fluid and adaptable.
7. Negotiate when the position is offered.
8. Be confident.
9. Develop a win/win atmosphere.
10. Identify all emotional aspects.
11. Keep the entire compensation package in mind.
12. Determine the real and potential values of your current package.
13. Choose your battles carefully.
14. Have them name the first figure.
15. Pause thirty seconds after repeating the initial offer.
16. Establish specific criteria for all bonuses/incentives.
17. Be prepared to walk away from the table.
18. Resell yourself.
19. Request the offer in writing (if there are unique aspects).
20. Ask for time (at least 24 hours) to consider an offer before accepting.

DON'Ts

1. Ask, "Is this offer negotiable?"
2. Name the first figure.
3. Accept the first offer.
4. Accept the offer on the spot.

5. Try to negotiate in the first interview.

6. Play "hard ball."

7. Allow your salary to be an albatross.

APPENDIX

BERNARD HALDANE ASSOCIATES NETWORK

As we noted previously, self-directed career books can help you become more effective with your job search. They outline useful principles, suggest effective strategies, and explain how you and others can achieve your own job and career success. That's our purpose in writing this and other books in the "Haldane's Best" series. We believe you can benefit greatly from the methods we have developed over the years and used successfully with hundreds of thousands of our clients.

We know the Haldane methods work because our clients are real cases of success that go far beyond the anecdotal. Indeed, our files are filled with unsolicited testimonials from former clients who have shared their insights into what really worked—evidence of our effectiveness in delivering what we promise our clients. We've shared some of these testimonials throughout the text of this book. What especially pleases us as career pro-

> ## Client Feedback
>
> *"You cannot ask questions of a book. You cannot get feedback on what to do from a book. And most of all, no book can help you with a job hunting campaign designed specifically for you. This is where Haldane comes in."*
> —J.A.C.
>
> *"I felt I could read a book or two on resumes and the world would beat a path to my door. What you did was to provide a step-by-step process for developing an effective marketing campaign."*
> —W.G.S.

fessionals is the fact that we've helped change the lives of so many people who have gone on to renewed career success. They discovered new opportunities that were a perfect fit for their particular interests, skills, and abilities. By focusing on their strengths and identifying their motivated skills and abilities, they were able to chart new and exciting career directions.

But our clients didn't achieve success overnight nor on their own. They worked with a structure, a schedule, and a vision of what they wanted to do next with their lives. Most important of all, they worked with a Career Advisor who helped them every step of the way. What we and other career specialists have learned over the years is no real secret, but it's worth repeating: most job seekers can benefit tremendously by working with a trained and experienced career professional who helps them complete each step of the career management process.

Our methods are not quick and easy, nor do they come naturally to most people—especially if you want to make the right career move. Many of our clients come to us after several weeks and months of frustrated efforts in conducting their own job search. Some tried doing everything according to the books, but they soon discovered that the books are only as good as the actions and outcomes that follow. What they most needed, and later appreciated, was a career professional whom they could work with in completing the critical assessment work (Success Factor Analysis) and in relating that key data to all other stages in their job search, from resume and letter writing to networking and interviewing. Using the proprietary Career Strategy 2000 electronic system, they gained access to a huge database of opportunities and employers. Once our clients decide to "do it the Haldane way" with a Career Advisor, they get surprising results. Again and again their testimonials emphasize the importance of completing Success Factor Analysis, developing a Haldane objective, networking, writing focused resumes and "T" letters, and interviewing and negotiating salary according to Haldane principles. Most important of all, they point out the value of having someone there—a Haldane Career Advisor—to guide them through the psychological ups and downs that often come with the highly ego-involved and rejection-ridden job finding process.

There's a season for everything, be it reading a self-directed career book or contacting a career professional for assistance. We've shared with you our insights and strategies by writing this book. Now it's up to you to take the next step. What you do next may make a critical difference in your career and your life. You may well discover your dream job on your own because you organized a Haldane-principled job search. If and when you feel you could benefit from the assistance of a career professional, please consider the Haldane network of Career Advisors. They have an exceptional track record of success based upon the methods outlined in this and other books in the "Haldane's Best" series. For your convenience, we've listed, along with contact information, the more than 80 offices that make up the Haldane network in the United States, Canada, and the United Kingdom. You can contact the office nearest you for more information and arrange for a free consultation. Please visit our Web site for additional information on Bernard Haldane Associates:

www.jobhunting.com

BERNARD HALDANE ASSOCIATES OFFICES

United States

ALABAMA:

10 Inverness Parkway, Suite 125
Birmingham, AL 35242
(205) 991-9134; Fax (205) 991-7164
bhaadm@aol.com

303 Williams Ave.; Suite 128
Huntsville, AL 35801
(256) 512-5559; Fax (256) 512-5564
bhahts@aol.com

ARIZONA:

3101 N. Central Avenue, Suite 1560
Phoenix, AZ 85012
(602) 248-8893; Fax (602) 248-8987
bhaphoenix@aol.com

5151 E. Broadway, Suite 750
Tucson, AZ 85711
(520) 790-2767; Fax (520) 790-2992
tucson@haldaneonline.com

CALIFORNIA:

1801 Avenue of the Stars, Suite 1011
Los Angeles, CA 90067
(310) 203-0955; Fax (310) 203-0933
careers@haldane.com

8801 Folsom Blvd., Suite 100
Sacramento, CA 95826
(916) 381-5094; Fax (916) 381-6506
bhasac@aol.com

8880 Rio San Diego Drive, Suite 300
San Diego, CA 92108
(619) 299-1424; Fax (619) 299-5340
sdbha@yahoo.com

388 Market Street, Suite 1600
San Francisco, CA 94111
(415) 391-8087; Fax (415) 391-4009
haldane@job-hunting.com

181 Metro Drive, Suite 410
San Jose, CA 95110-1346
(408) 437-9200; Fax (408) 437-1300
haldane@job-hunting.com

Pacific Plaza, Suite 220
1340 Treat Blvd.
Walnut Creek, CA 94596
(925) 945-0776; Fax (925) 939-3764
haldane@job-hunting.com

COLORADO:

The Registry, 1113 Spruce Street
Boulder, CO 80302
(303) 571-1757; Fax (303) 825-5900
jobhunt@haldane.com

Plaza of the Rockies,
111 S. Tejon Street, Suite 610
Colorado Springs, CO 80903-2263
(719) 634-8000; Fax (719) 635-8008
springs@haldane.com

1625 Broadway, #2550
Denver, CO 80202
(303) 825-5700; Fax (303) 825-5900
jobhunt@haldane.com

Denver Technological Center
8400 E. Prentice Ave., Suite 301
Englewood, CO 80111
(303) 793-3800, Fax (303) 793-3040
jobhunt@haldane.com

Poudre Valley Center
1075 W. Horsetooth Road, Suite 204
Fort Collins, CO 80526
(970) 223-5459; Fax (970) 226-2757
poudre@haldane.com

CONNECTICUT:

State House Square
Six Central Row
Hartford, CT 06103-2701
(860) 247-7500; Fax (860) 247-1213
hartford@haldane.com

FLORIDA:

6622 Southpoint Dr. So., Suite 340
Jacksonville, FL 32216
(904) 296-6802; Fax (904) 296-3506
haldane340@msn.com

901 North Lake Destiny Drive,
Suite 379
Maitland, FL 32751 **(Orlando)**
(407) 660-8323; Fax (407) 660-2434
bhaorlando@aol.com

5100 W. Kennedy Blvd., Suite 425
Tampa, FL 33609
(813) 287-1393; Fax (813) 289-4125
haldane@worldnet.att.net

GEORGIA:

4170 Ashford Dunwoody Road,
Suite 575
Atlanta, GA 30319
(404) 255-3184; Fax (404) 250-1165
haldane@mindspring.com

ILLINOIS:

One Magnificent Mile
980 N. Michigan Ave., Suite 1400
Chicago, IL 60611
(312) 214-4920; Fax (312) 214-7674
jobs@bhaldane.com

One Tower Lane, Suite 1700
Oakbrook Terrace, IL 60181
(630) 573-2923; Fax (630) 574-7048
jobs@bhaldane.com

1901 N. Roselle Road, Suite 800
Schaumburg, IL 60195
(847) 490-6454; Fax (847) 490-6529
jobs@bhaldane.com

INDIANA:

8888 Keystone Crossing, Suite 1675
Indianapolis, IN 46240
(317) 846-6062; Fax (317) 846-6354
bha_indy_admn@worldnet.att.net

IOWA:

6165 NW 86th Street
Johnston, IA 50131 **(Des Moines)**
(515) 727-1623; Fax (515) 727-1673
jobs@bhaldane.com

KANSAS:

7007 College Blvd., Suite 727
Overland Park, KS 66211
(913) 327-0300; Fax (913) 327-7067
mail@kchaldane.com

2024 N. Woodlawn, Suite 402
Wichita, KS 67208
(316) 687-5333; Fax (316) 689-6924
mail@wkhaldane.com

KENTUCKY:

330 E. Main Street, Suite 200
Lexington, KY 40507
(606) 255-2163; Fax (606) 231-0737
bha_lex_admn@worldnet.att.net

9100 Shelbyville Rd., Suite 280
Louisville, KY 40222
(502) 326-5121; Fax (502) 426-5348
bha_louis_admn@worldnet.att.net

MAINE:

477 Congress Street, 5th Floor
Portland, ME 04101-3406
(207) 772-1700; Fax (207) 772-7117
jobhunting@haldane.com

MASSACHUSETTS:

277 Dartmouth St.
Boston, MA 02116-2800
(617) 247-2500; Fax (617) 247-7171
jobhunting@haldane.com

10 Mechanic Street
Worcester, MA 01608
(508) 791-6900; Fax (508) 791-6901
jobhunting@haldane.com

MICHIGAN:

5777 West Maple Rd., Suite 190
West Bloomfield, MI 48322
(Detroit)
(248) 737-4700; Fax (248) 737-4789
bhadet@coast.net

MINNESOTA:

3433 Broadway St., N.E., Suite 440
Minneapolis, MN 55413
(612) 378-0600; Fax (612) 378-9225
jobs@bhaldane.com

MISSOURI:

680 Craig Road, Suite 400
St. Louis, MO 63141
(314) 991-5444; Fax (314) 991-5207
careers@haldanestl.com

NEBRASKA:

12020 Shamrock Plaza, Suite 200
Omaha, NE 68154
(402) 330-9461; Fax (402) 330-9847
omaha@haldanestl.com

NEW HAMPSHIRE:

20 Trafalgar Square, Suite 452
Nashua, NH 03063
(603) 886-4200; Fax (603) 886-4242
jobhunting@haldane.com

NEW JERSEY:

The Atrium, E. 80 Route 4,
Suite 110
Paramus, NJ 07652
(201) 587-9898; Fax (201) 587-9119
jobs@bhaldane.com

100 Princeton Overlook Center,
Suite 100
Princeton, NJ 08540
(609) 987-0400; Fax (609) 987-0011
jobs@bhaldane.com

NEW YORK:

80 State Street, 11th Floor
Albany, NY 12207
(518) 447-1000; Fax (518) 447-0011
jobhunting@haldane.com

838 Crosskey Office Park
Fairport, NY 14450 **(Rochester)**
(716) 425-0550; Fax (716) 425-0554
haldane@frontiernet.net

261 Madison Avenue, Suite 1504
New York, NY 10016
(212) 490-7799; Fax (212) 490-1712
jobs@bhaldane.com

300 International Drive, Suite 213
Williamsville, NY 14221
(Buffalo)
(716) 626-3400; Fax (716) 626-3402
jobhunting@haldane.com

Thurway Office Building
290 Elwood Davis Road
Liverpool, NY 13088 **(Syracuse)**
(817) 425-0550; Fax (315) 641-2677
haldane@frontiernet.net

50 Charles Lindbergh Blvd., Suite 400
Uniondale, NY 11553 **(Long Island)**
(516) 390-4780; Fax (516) 390-4871
jobs@bhaldane.com

NORTH CAROLINA:

6100 Fairview Road, Suite 355
Charlotte, NC 28210
(704) 643-5959; Fax (704) 556-1674
charlotte@haldanestl.com

4011 West Chase Blvd., Suite 210
Raleigh, NC 27607
(919) 546-9759; Fax (919) 546-9766
raleigh@haldanestl.com

OHIO:

3250 W. Market Street, Suite 307
Akron, OH 44333
(330) 867-7889; Fax (330) 867-7874
gcmg_hq@worldnet.att.net

625 Eden Park Drive, Suite 775
Cincinnati, OH 45202
(513) 621-4440; Fax (513) 562-8943
bha_cincy_admn@worldnet.att.net

6500 Rockside Rd., Suite 180
Cleveland, OH 44131
(216) 447-0166 ; Fax (216) 447-0015
bha_clev_admn@worldnet.att.net

111 West Rich Street, Suite 480
Columbus, OH 43215
(614) 224-2322; Fax (614) 224-2333
bha_colb_admn@worldnet.att.net

Fifth Third Center
110 N. Main Street, Suite 1280
Dayton, OH 45402
(937) 224-5279; Fax (937) 224-5284
bha_dayton_admn@worldnet.att.net

3131 Executive Parkway, Suite 300
Toledo, OH 43606
(419) 535-3898; Fax (419) 531-4771
bhadet@coast.net

OKLAHOMA:

3030 NW Expressway, Suite 727
Oklahoma City, OK 73112
(405) 948-7668; Fax (405) 948-7869
bhaokc@telepath.com

7060 South Yale, Suite 707
Tulsa, OK 74136
(918) 491-9151; Fax (918) 491-9153
bhatulsa@swbell.net

OREGON:

1220 SW Morrison, Suite 800
Portland, OR 97205
(503) 295-5926; Fax (503) 295-2639
bhacareers@aol.com

PENNSYLVANIA:

Parkview Tower
1150 First Avenue, Suite 385
King of Prussia, PA 19404
(Philadelphia)
(610) 491-9050; Fax (610) 491-9080
jobs@bhaldane.com

Three Gateway Center, 18 East
401 Liberty Avenue
Pittsburgh, PA 15222
(412) 263-5627; Fax (412) 263-2027
bhapittspa@aol.com

RHODE ISLAND:

1400 Bank Boston Plaza
Providence, RI 02903
(401) 461-9900; Fax (401) 461-0099
jobhunting@haldane.com

SOUTH CAROLINA:

5000 Thurmond Mall, Suite 106
Columbia, SC 29201
(803) 799-9155; Fax (803) 799-9163
columbia@haldanestl.com

TENNESSEE:

7610 Gleason Drive, Suite 301
Knoxville, TN 37919
(423) 690-6767; Fax (423) 690-3990
bhaknox@worldnet.att.net

3150 Lennox Park Blvd., Suite 302
Memphis, TN 38115
(901) 375-1111; Fax (901) 375-1545
memphis@haldanestl.com

424 Church Street, Suite 1625
Nashville, TN 37219
(615) 742-8440; Fax (615) 742-8445
jobs@bhaldane.com

TEXAS:

Park Central VII, 12750 Merit Dr.,
Ste. 200
Dallas, TX 75251
(972) 503-4100; (Fax) 972-503-4445
bhadfw@ont.com

UTAH:

215 South State Street, Suite 200
Salt Lake City, UT 84111
(801) 355-4242; Fax (801) 355-3238
mail@slchaldane.com

VIRGINIA:

2101 Wilson Blvd., Suite 950
Arlington, VA 22201 **(DC)**
(703) 516-9122; Fax (703) 812-3001
jobs@bhaldane.com

6800 Paragon Place, Suite 106
Richmond, VA 23230
(804) 282-0470; Fax (804) 282-1983
jobs@bhaldane.com

WASHINGTON:

10900 N.E. 8th St., Suite 1122
Bellevue, WA 98004 **(Seattle)**
(425) 462-7308; Fax (425) 462-9670
careerspnw@aol.com

West 818 Riverside Drive, Suite 320
Spokane, WA 99201
(509) 325-7650; Fax (509) 325-7655
careersspo@aol.com

Tacoma Security Building
917 Pacific Avenue, Suite 400
Tacoma,WA 98402
(253) 383-8757; Fax (253) 383-0887
careersadv@aol.com

WISCONSIN:

4351 West College Ave., Suite 215
Appleton, WI 54914
(920) 831-7820; Fax (920) 831-7831
bhaappletn@aol.com

15800 W. Bluemound Road,
Suite 320
Brookfield, WI 53005
(Milwaukee)
(414) 797-8055; Fax (414) 797-9002
bhamilw@aol.com

5315 Wall Street, Suite 220
Madison, WI 53718
(608) 246-2100; Fax (608) 246-2031
bhamadison@aol.com

Canada:

3027 Harvester Rd., Suite 105
Burlington, Ontario, Canada
L7N 3G7
(905) 681-0180; Fax (905) 681-0181
haldane@bserv.com

Suite 3000, 30th Floor
Petro Canada Centre, West Tower
156th Ave. SW

Calgary, Alberta, Canada T2P3Y7
(403) 265-1372; Fax (403) 265-1382
bha@portal.ca

One London Place,
255 Queens Avenue, Suite 2150
London, Ontario, Canada N6A 5R8
(519) 439-2580; Fax (519) 439-2587
bhaldane@netcom.ca

1250 Blvd. Rene-Levesque Ouest,
Suite 2335
Montreal, Quebec, Canada
H3B 4W8
(514) 938-0578; Fax (514) 938-9165
bhaldane@bha.attcanada.net

Manulife Place
55 Metcalfe Street, Suite 1460
Ottawa, Ontario, Canada K1P 6L5
(613) 234-2530; Fax (613) 234-2560
bhaottawa@aol.com

One Financial Place
One Adelaide Street East, Suite 2201
Toronto, Ontario, Canada
M5C 2V9
(416) 363-9241; Fax (416) 363-9246
bhatoronto@aol.com

IBM Tower, Suite 1800
701 West Georgia Street
Vancouver, British Columbia
V7Y 1C6
(604) 609-6661; Fax (604) 609-2638
bha@portal.ca

United Kingdom:

Cornwall Court
19 Cornwall Street
Birmingham B3 2DY UK
011-44-1212-243192;
Fax 011-44-1212-243282
bhamidlands@haldane.co.uk

2440 The Quadrant
Aztec West
Almondsbury, **Bristol** BS32
4AQ UK
011-44-1454-878506;
Fax 011-44-1454-878606
bhabristol@haldane.co.uk

Marcol House
289/293 Regent Street
London W1R 7PD UK
011-44-1712-909100;
Fax 011-44-1712-909109
bha@haldane.co.uk

82 King Street
Manchester M2 4QW UK
011-44-1619-358070;
(Fax) 011-44-1619-358217
bhanorth@aol.com

INDEX

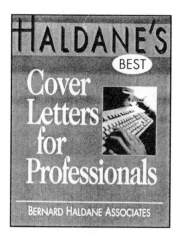